Now You Know

Guide

FLAVIO SOUZA

DEDICATION

Well, as this is not a biography nor a novel but a guide,
let's keep it simple, shall we?

To all Lovely Intelligent Netizen…

CONTENTS

ACKNOWLEDGMENTS

The Now You Know Guide kickoff through crowdfunding and I would like to give a special thank you for all the backers of this project:

(Alphabetic Order)
A super thanks goes to:

Madeleine Thom
Naoko Machida

As they bought multiple copies and believed in this project from day one. Thank you very much.

Furthermore, I would like to extend my sincere thanks to all the other knights that also pledged for this project:

Albinas Zakarauskas, Alejandro Garcia, Amy Wienecke, Andreas Sollund, Andy Laver, Arnold Mascarenhas, Arun Kumar, Attila Odry, Bran- don Redding, Corey Fleischer, Ed Warcholak, Eduardo Ibacache Rodriguez, Fabien Fontaine Gerrit Ophey, Gretchen Shinoda, Jan Eveleens, Ken Taylor, Kishori Prabhu, Leon Herbert, Naswell Watson, Sergio Lopez Figueroa, Symon Peters and Yogev Gavri.

DISCLAIMER

Okay - we all dislike these things, but you know how it is these days, we need to make sure we are on the same page here: First off - let me say this - if you are looking for a 138-page guidebook that will make you a million dollars in 15 minutes online... Wrong book!

This guidebook has been written to provide information about online marketing (in a very broad sense, not really focusing on a particular channel). Every effort has been made to make the Now You Know Guide as complete and accurate as possible. However, there may be mistakes in typography or content.

Hello, Lawyers! The purpose of this guide is to educate. The author does not warrant that the information in this guide is complete and shall not be responsible for any errors or omissions. The author and publisher shall have neither liability nor responsibility to any person or entity regarding any loss or damage caused or alleged to be caused directly or indirectly by this guidebook.

All information contained herein is for entertainment only. The authors of this product assume no liability, legally, financially or otherwise, for any results or consequences of using any information in this guide or any other products that may have been received as bonuses or additional materials. No claims are made on earnings, future, current or past, by the author, nor are any guarantees or promises made.

A SHORT INTRO:

What a long, odd trip it's been for marketing.

In America, the first magazines were published in 1741, the first billboards in the late 1800s and the first-ever ad (for Bulova watches) in 1941.

Now, it might sound strange that I wrote marketing and not advertisement on the line above, but remember that "advertising" is only one component of the overall marketing process.

The best analogy to understand the difference between marketing and advertisement is to see marketing as a big extra-large pepperoni pizza, the whole marketing is the pizza itself, and each slice will be a marketing component such as advertising, market research, media planning, public relations, community relations, customer support, and sales strategy…

Advertising, while the most visible slice of the pizza, is still only one slice of the marketing pizza. So, in the old days of marketing (beginning of the last century), marketing as a process had the main goal to get the public's attention and spinning that into sales.

Often this meant companies embraced a bazooka strategy "sell- as-much-as-we-can" approach with little or no concern for building long-term relationships.

"Buster Guru," a site that claims to be "the king of funny marketing quotes," has a better marketing description:

"Marketing is about telling one story in a thousand different magical ways, and here's that story: Your life could be better, and once you buy what we're offering, it will be better. The end".

- Buster Guru

But somewhere around the 1950s things changed, companies saw that old ways of selling were wearing thin with customers.

As competition grew stiffer across most industries, organizations looked to the buyer side of the transaction for ways to improve. What they found was an emerging philosophy suggesting that the key factor in successful marketing is understanding the needs of customers.

This now-famous Marketing Concept suggests decisions made by marketers should follow a premise: FIRST know your customers and what they want. Only then should you (or an organization) initiate developing and marketing goods and services.

So, marketers have learned they can no longer limit their marketing effort to just getting customers to purchase more. They must understand who their customers are and what they want.

Then Steve Jobs (from Apple's golden days) came along and said the now-famous phrase:

"Some people say, "Give the customers what they want." But that's not my approach. Our job is to figure out what they're going to want before they do. I think Henry Ford once said, "If I'd asked customers what they wanted, they would have told me, 'A faster horse!'" People don't know what they want until you show it to them. That's why I never rely on market research. Our task is to read things that are not yet on the page."

Fast forward to today, marketing continues to evolve, and it has changed rapidly over centuries and will continue to do so.

As any good marketer, you should know that changes are particularly impacted by the Political, Economic, Social, Technological, Legal and Environmental factors (the famous **PESTLE analysis**), I actually like to rearrange the order as Social, Legal, Economic-Environmental (combining those two), Political and Technological (hence the mnemonic SLEPT), which is easier to memorize …

Putting in another word, if you miss these factors,

you <u>SLEPT</u>…

So, thanks to the technology improvements (from portable devices to the internet itself), new social behaviors were born and community-driven sites like Instagram and Twitter (just to mention two) flourished, so as today, marketing seems to be going "online" big time…

And online opens new possibilities to communication and it improves the way people connect and buy. And having realized the large number of people that log in to internet sites daily, modern marketers found a new marketing channel for building a relationship with their crowd.

Today, online in general is no longer just an ingenious way for people to meet, connect and share. It is now also one of the most powerful tools which anyone can use to build their own targeted market niche/listener's channel.

However, it is noteworthy that social media marketing is like a double-edged sword – it needs to be wielded correctly. In the hands of a skilled marketer, it is an effective channel. But in the hands of an amateur, it can turn success into demise.

So, to help you avoid the pitfalls of "marketing online", I made a list of 101 tips that will guide you to enhance your presence online and build your own direct channels with your consumers/listeners.

The Now You Know Guidebook tries to give you practical and good tips, but you have to really want it and implement to see the results.

My goal in writing the Now You Know Guidebook is to focus on the useful and doable info and discard any page filler.

Therefore, I divided this guide in two very simple parts:

The first part is **WHO ARE YOU (NOW)?**

It means your present time and your present image; the idea is to have an accurate snapshot of your present stage on your online endeavor.

We need to create your honesty credibility online as time goes by, and without this part (being honest on your current phase), all your efforts will be lost.

The second part of the guide will help you to move to **WHO WOULD YOU WANT TO BE OR WHAT DO YOU WANT TO ACHIEVE (IN THE FUTURE).**

What I see online these days, are people trying to work (from the beginning) on the image of what they want to be (a short cut) completing ignoring the first part of this guide (Who are you (now)), and by doing so, people are missing the work on the credibility and that miss will destroy their efforts in the short-long term.

Note: Through the book, when you see the pronoun "You", what I really mean is the individual reader or your company/brand/services/products…Remember that when you keep absorbing the ideas and doing the actions (exercises).

Finally, this guide is a perfect match when you are in front of your computer, tablet or/and smartphone. The idea is to implement those learnings and not just read it. I made it compact and easy to carry it around with a single goal in mind: I want YOU to use it!

Do all the actions (exercises); perhaps you can get a simple notepad (or use a computer soft or a tablet app) for keeping everything organized and in handy.

This will be important later when you review your notes and tasks as you progress through the Now You Know Guide.

So, read on (just like you would do it in a novel, cover to cover and without jumping pages), and I will show you how you can turn the online world into your advantage and build your own success online and probably offline too.

what people think it looks like

what it really looks like

WHO ARE YOU (NOW)?

I would like to start this chapter by talking about some principles of marketing you need to be aware of to successfully build your online presence.

Although I am also a professor on the subject, I promise you not to turn this chapter in an academic lecture about marketing. Instead, I would like to focus in just one specific strategy you have to know before anything else …

So, without further delay here goes: **POSITIONING**:

According to the Wikipedia:

"Positioning refers to the place that a brand occupies in the minds of the customers and how it is distinguished from the products of the competitors. In order to position products or brands, companies may emphasize the distinguishing features of their brand (what it is, what it does and how, etc.) or they may try to create a suitable image (inexpensive or premium, utilitarian or luxurious, entry-level or high-end, etc.) through the marketing mix. Once a brand has achieved a strong position, it can become difficult to reposition it."

So, in our case, let's replace the word "brand" and add "YOU" or "Yourself as brand", so the idea is the same and needs to be done before anything else.

YOU need to find and craft your positioning online, and that positioning must be true to who you are now.

HOW? You might ask.

Well, marketing again comes in hand and I would like to share with you 3 simple steps to help you in discovering your best and honesty positioning online.

(Note: Don't even think to skip those 3 steps as it's important now and even more later)

STEP #1 - FREE PERSONALITY ANALYSIS

This free personality test is based on Carl Jung's and Isabel Briggs Myers' personality type theory and can help you to discover more about yourself:

https://www.16personalities.com/free-personality-test

Most times, we think we know everything about ourselves but actually, we don't, so by doing this test, you will have a good sense on how you stand with yourself.

(Note: If the link happens to not work, just google "16 personalities" or "free personality test" It's free to take the test, so do not go to sites that charge for the test.)

STEP #2 - THE SWOT ANALYSIS

Start with a simple SWOT analysis of yourself…

Most of you might be already familiar with SWOT analysis, but if you are screeching your head and thinking what the heck is a SWOT analysis? I will give you a SWOT 101 crash course below:

SWOT stands for Strengths, Weaknesses, Opportunities, and Threats.

So, SWOT analysis is basically a framework used to evaluate a business's competitive position by identifying its strengths, weaknesses, opportunities and threats. However, in our particular case, we will use this framework to evaluate yourself against the other people/competitors online.

Strength – These are the areas you have an advantage edge (i.e., talents, skill sets, capabilities, etc. Think on what makes you unique or things you can do better than the average Joe)

Weakness – These are the areas you need improvement on or that there are other people who can do tasks better than you. (Be honest with yourself when you are filling this part out)

Opportunity – These are the possibilities where you can take advantage of, or where your talents, skills, and capabilities can flourish, which leads to the achievement of your dreams, goals, and ambitions.

And finally…

Threats – These prevent or keeps you from achieving your dreams and goals.

If that is not straight forward for you, you can ask yourself these questions:

Strengths:

1. Can you define yourself in one word or ability? What do you do best?
2. What are your positive personality traits? Your comfortable zone?
3. What do other people see as your strengths? (Avoid just asking your mom on this one thou)
4. What do you have in your advantage (skills, education, networks, etc.)?
5. What other skills make you stand out from the rest?
6. What resources do you have? (Money, time, etc.)
7. What is your greatest achievement, the one you are proudest about it?
8. What personal core values do you have that may help you reach your goals?

Suggestion: The "stand out from the rest" part is key here in strengths. For example, to say you have "Integrity" (honesty) is not a unique strength, because everyone else has (until proved contrary) but if you add "Bravery" into it and say "I am willing to fight for a more honesty world "then that might be a different story.

Weaknesses:

1. What tasks do you avoid doing because of a lack of confidence or knowledge?
2. What personality traits may be holding you back in your career? Your uncomfortable zone?
3. What disadvantages do you have? (Skills, education, networks, etc.)?
4. What fears do you have that may be holding you back?
5. What are your negative habits or traits? (Laziness, lack of focus, etc.)
6. What resources are you lacking? (*Don't say money :)*
7. In what areas do you need more training or education?

Again, be honest and realistic when answering the questions. It's a self-assessment which only you will see. Use it as a stepping stone for future improvements.

Opportunities:

1. How can you turn your strengths into opportunities?
2. How can you turn your weaknesses into opportunities?
3. Is there a need in your department that no one is meeting?
4. What could you do today that isn't being done?
5. How is your field changing? How can you take advantage of those changes?
6. What new technology may help you meet your goals?
7. Do you have contacts that could help you?

Suggestion: It's great if an opportunity matches your strengths. But sometimes great opportunities arise in areas that don't match your skill set. Consider the pros and cons before disregarding them.

Threats:

1. What obstacles do you face?
2. Could any of your weaknesses prevent you from succeeding?
3. Do any of your strengths hold you back?
4. Is your job (life, health, etc.) changing?
5. Do you have any obligations (work or otherwise) that may limit your development?
6. Are you competing with others for what you want?
7. Are there changes in your field or in technology that could threaten your success?

Suggestion: When it comes to eliminating threats, one of the easiest to fix is negative personality traits. Get professional help if necessary. For example, if time management is an issue, you can hire a productivity coach.

Now you know how to do it, it's time to create your own personal SWOT analysis diagram.

You can get a blank personal SWOT analysis template online (https://creately.com/templates/), or you can just grab a blank paper and write down your Strengths, Weaknesses, Opportunities, and Threats.

The important thing here is to do it, no excuses to not do so.

STEP #3 - THE MIND MAPS

Mind maps are visual tools used in strategic planning to show how various items relate to each other. A mind map is a diagram that presents words, ideas or images linked to an initial central theme or idea.

Mind maps are a form of brainstorming and was popularized by psychologist Tony Buzan in 1976, according to the University of Surrey.

Ever feel like you have too many thoughts floating around in your head? Then mapping them out could be just what you need. Mind maps help you to brainstorm, take notes or work through complex problems.

This exercise helps bring your ideas to life by creating a visual organization of your thoughts so you can remember, identify correlations, and see the big picture.

The process starts with an initial question or problem written in the center of a large piece of paper or on a whiteboard. In our case here is:

WHO ARE YOU (NOW)?

Additional ideas or concepts are then tied to and branched out from the central idea.

Again, you can get a mind map template online (https://templatelab.com/mind-map/) or you can just grab a blank paper and write down.

After taking the 3 steps, you will be better off to understand who are you now.

101 ACTIONS, HERE WE GO:

BEFORE POSTING ANYTHING...

'There is no elevator to success, you have to take the stairs'

Zig Ziglar

1 DEFINING YOUR GOALS

It's the first step in anything in life, right? Well, it should be.

For instance, ask yourself where do you want to arrive on marketing yourself online... I mean, are you looking for fame or for making money or both. Whatever it is, **you have to** be crystal clear on where do you want to arrive.

The goal(s) must adhere to the S.M.A.R.T method — they **need to** be: Specific, Measurable, Attainable, Relevant and Time-based.

Why do that: Well, to minimize wasted efforts and time, and mostly important to keep YOU (or your brand) focused.

A focused goal gives us crucial directions or otherwise we will end up our life just stuck in a mental loop that might include questions like "Wait a minute, if I just got out the shower clean then how come my towel get dirty?"

ACTION: Write down your initial goal(s) for your online journey: You can do it by set smalls daily goals (milestones to do it) or/and a big goal you want to achieve by going online. It essential to have clear objectives set on. Examples of goals can vary a lot and it is personal but here go **some** examples: Build meaningful connections online, begin partnerships that will help you to move from who you are now to who you want to be (future), construct a strong presence online and leverage on that for e-commerce or starting your own business...If you already have an online presence you should conduct a social media audit and see if **you need to** do adjustments or start from scratch.

2 ALIGN GOALS WITH METRICS

Realize your goals for your online journey is a great first step, now it is time to think how you will know when you reach them. As Jayson DeMers (EmailAnalytics Founder) advises, "First you need to know what to measure. The end goals dictate the measurement metric."

He offers some metrics for four online common goals:

- *"If you're looking to generate traffic, your metric should be: unique visitors from social websites where you've run your social media campaigns".*
- *"If you're looking to create a following, your metric should be: subscribers, followers on your social channels (Instagram, YouTube, etc.)".*
- *"If you're looking to generate interaction, your metric should be: quantity and type of commentary (Facebook comments, Twitter replies / mentions)".*
- *"If you're looking to generate revenue (which is the ultimate purpose), your metric should be: the precise dollar value of every lead a social post generates".*

Keep this information in mind when crafting your quantifiable metrics that will go along with your plan. The metrics here will work like a compass that helps sailors to find their location and to know which direction to go to reach their destination.

ACTION: Create a list of measurement metrics for each of your goals you defined on idea #01, you can also use time as one parameter for your goals, for example by 2024, I want to complete these goals…

3 ONLINE PRESENCE MUST FIT

Decide on your online presence so it fits your goals and personality.

You want people to find you all over the online world: In all forums, chat rooms, social media sites… And that is so true, especially on those corners of the net where your target market is. However, as you realized after the previous 3 steps exercises on PART 1 - WHO ARE YOU (NOW)?

There are online places that do not fit with your own personality or even beliefs or lifestyle.

For example, I am not a guy for Instagram as I actually post very few selfies online, I like to keep a low profile as I value my privacy and that's also the reason I gave up on Facebook. Anyway, there is no perfect online place on the net, you need to do some compromises and choose the one you feel will work the best for you and your goals.

But some choices are pretty straight forward based on your initial goal, let's say you want to be a famous YouTuber in the future, well, better start now developing your YouTube channel then.

So, my point is that not all online sites are for you. Choose wise where do you fit on the web and work your way up.

***

ACTION: Write down a list of all possible online presence you can think of (forums, directory listings, messaging apps, social media sites …) Now write down their PRO and CONS according to your own personality. Go and rank them all based on your goals.

4 STUDY YOUR TARGETING

Plenty of people join social media sites.

However, you do not really want to target them all (we already talk about this on the previous idea #3) mainly because your offerings will not be for everybody anyway.

Most people think the ultimate goal online is to acquire "followers" or build a very broad target. Some even believe that many followers work as some kind of validation of their character or magically generate trust among other users. Wrong! A famous internet quote nails down this thought:

"The number of "FOLLOWERS" you have doesn't make you better than anyone else Adolph Hitler had millions and Jesus had only 12." – Unknown

Therefore, you need to focus on a group of people which are "potential REAL "LISTENERS" to your message" and if you can resonate or has something in common with them, it's even better.

Your holy grail quest is to find those users. Now, remember that everything in life changes (included your "targets"), therefore, even if you are set down in a couple of targets, keep an eye open for new targets that might appear as time goes by.

ACTION: Study the online platform you are joining, try to identify your initial listeners (users with similar thoughts / tastes…), then analyze the tone of their posts, what kind of posts attracted the most comments (forget about likes, check interactions) Take notes on that.

5 A QUALITY PROFILE

First, if you want to use any online presence (especially in social media) you need to have a quality profile.

Your profile needs to introduce you in 30 secs or less; it needs to answer the simple question: Who are you (now)?

Let the people who view your profile page know who you really are and give an idea of what you do or have to offer them. Put effort into your personal and business profile on all your online presence.

Don't just throw something up there, even if you think you'll go back later and make it better. Someone might see your profile today, and the first impression you make might not be a good one and boom! You've lost a likely "listener".

(Note: I prefer the term: "listeners" instead of followers, because I believe anyone can have followers, but only few can build real listeners online, listeners here mean that an online user is really "inner listening" your message).

ACTION: You will need a clean background profile picture (use the picture you feel more comfortable with, it need not be your latest picture but do not choose one too old), the picture needs to fit who you are now. After you decide on the picture, you need to craft a great intro/headline, this should be unique and must come from you (not from me) needs to be genuine and show your own personality, try it first and as you continue to advance through this guide, you will get a better picture on how to improve it later.

6 DO & DON'TS ON PROFILE:

Expanding a bit on the previous idea #5, here is a quick guideline for profiles that can help you (or your brand) to build a solid and trustable profile.

DO:

Turn your summary into a story (your story, make it personal and unique. Showcase your passion).

Highlight your qualities / skills / uniqueness /services / your offer … Keep it simple and attractive and focused on who you are now.

DON'T:

Copy someone's profile

Lie about yourself or your achievements (That's a never)

Go into many details

Overuse on buzzwords (your profile should be focused on humans not on SEO / algorithms reading)

Make a profile based on who you want to be (future)

ACTION: Pretty straight forward. Craft the DOs above on a piece of paper and double check on the don'ts.

7 PLANNING YOUR CONTENTS

Getting started without a posting / idea plan can lead to a messy start. This will not be good for you (or your service / product / brand).

So, before you post or market yourself online, plan for contents.

For example, image a YouTuber that just turns on the camera and start talking, it may get somewhere in the first couple of videos, but after that "novelty" period wears off, it will probably be boring/ repetitive to its audience.

In my particular case, I have decided to position myself as an entrepreneur, so initially my contents / posts were just around this theme.

Later on, I have learned via (trial and error) that a humor approach would be beneficial for my goals, so I added that in as well.

So, you need to plan for at least two weeks (ideal a month) of contents in advance so you can have a safety buffer if you run out of ideas for your posts.

ACTION: Write down at least 2 weeks of posts ideas in advance. You need to have some buffer for when you reach a wall on your creativity, therefore planning in advance is always a good idea. Stick with your positioning. Remember, you are trying to let people know who you are, building trust is the goal on this phase, so avoid odd posts at this stage, play safe, but you also have to be bold in other to cut through the online noise, more on that topic later.

8 THE 80% / 20% RULE

As you are developing your content, I would like to share with you a golden rule that works well for me.

It's the 80%/20% content rule:

I have learned (especially initially where you are building trust and trying to get noticing online) that if you apply this 80/20 rule, your number of listeners will gradually increase, and you will be noticed.

Ok, what 80% stands for… 80% of your posts should be focused on HELPING others online.

What do I mean with that? Well, 80% of your posts should not be about yourself, should be about others.

For example, you can share something that uplifts the mood of someone or share some knowledge that will resonate with your target. Think about "unconditional love" you are just giving away without thinking of any return or prize for yourself.

Now because "unconditional love" does not pay the bills, you have the other 20% to make up for that gap. So, 20% of your posts can be focused on what you are offering or selling.

ACTION: Go back to your 2 weeks of post ideas you just made on idea #7 and check if those posts are guided by 80%/20% rule; if not, replace those unbalancing the content rule. Your goal is to have 80% "giveaways" and 20% "sales pitches".

9 NOT ONLY TEXT

If all your posts are just words and sentences, it will soon get boring no matter how interesting your posts are. This is true even for a tweet.

So sometimes, try to convey what you want to say through videos, images, and presentations.

You must screen videos for possibly offensive elements. Never ever post or share someone else's video without watching it until the end. Always judge by yourself if that particular video will help with your positioning and your goals.

Images (just like videos) should also be unique, don't share it just because it went viral or someone famous shared. Remember, you have to craft a positioning among your target, not amplifying some else's positioning.

The only exception here should be when the viral image or video helps others online. If so, then velocity in sharing is everything because you want to be seeing as that unique person that always has the freshest content.

ACTION: Check how many of your 2 weeks' contents could you convert to visual (video, image, presentation …) if you can convert most it is a good sign, but if you cannot convert any, it is better to go back to the drawing board again and generate more ideas with images/videos in mind. The best scenario is to have a 50%/50% split between word posts and visual posts.

10 TONE AND LANGUAGE

Use appropriate tone and language that suits your online outlet choice, your positioning, and your own personality. Again, you have to be true to yourself.

However, you need to try to adapt to your chosen online outlet as well as your positioning niche without trading off your own personality and skills (more about that later).

Let's say you are an "introvert" but chose to join Instagram or TikTok as your main online presence just because they are a hot place to be nowadays.

Well, not a really good match there as most of Instagram pictures or stories are done outdoors or in groups, and making TikTok videos for an introvert has the same effect as attending a baseball game alone and see your face get aired by mistake on "the kiss cam" during the game.

As the goal in this phase is to build your credibility online, you have to pick up the tone and language that is more natural for you and fit that within your online outlet.

ACTION: As you already conducted research about your online platform, I believe you already got a fair idea about the tone and language the users are using there. So, your action here is to innovate on the online platform you chose to be by being more creative with- out changing the tone or language level in the platform. Basically, brainstorm on your head (be creative), and find new approaches that are unique but still a fit to your online outlet choice, positioning, and own personality.

11 ONE VOICE, ONE TONE

Expanding on the idea #10, your message should be focused but adaptable for your different online outlets without losing its essence (core message).

That will create a single voice, and it is very beneficial for attracting the right set of "listeners" in your direction, people who resonate with that one voice (your message).

Now regarding tones, some writers will suggest you use different tones (or adapt your tone in a way to fit a particular online outlet you use); I call that a big mistake, because then you are giving up on being yourself, and making the mistake to create a "fake tone" to be easily acceptable by the group you are in, and in the long run you risk losing your credibility when your real tone surface.

When I got into LinkedIn, people were harsh commenting *"this is not Facebook, keep your humor out of here"* and it is very easier (and dangerous) to change your natural tone (I am a funny guy, what can I do? Should I swallow "UnProzac" pills for going online?).

What I have discovered is those people that were unsympathetic were not my "listeners" target anyway. I always want to attract people with a positive behavior towards life. So, one voice and one natural tone always…

ACTION: Get 5 of your posts ideas and rewrite them playing with 3 personality traits you may have, examples of personality traits: Adventurous, Helpful, Affable, Humble, Capable, Imaginative, Charming, Impartial, Confident, Independent, Discreet, Optimistic, Dutiful, Persistent, Precise, Fearless, Sociable …

12 BE PRECISE AND BRIEF

People hate to read lengthy posts. Some people are just very busy, so we can't really blame them.

So, with that in mind, you must keep posts and comments brief and concise. That's another advantage for using visuals as support on what you want to convey or say.

One picture is worth a thousand words or millions if it is from a famous photographer :) Don't believe me? Search photographer: Andreas Gursky and his picture of the Rhine River that was sold for 4.3 million dollars.

Anyway, the U.S. Navy in 1960 had a design principle called: "The KISS principle" a famous acronym for "keep it simple, stupid" or "keep it stupid simple"

As it's a common belief that most systems work best if they are kept simple rather than made complicated; therefore, simplicity should be a key goal in design, and unnecessary complexity should be avoided, the U.S. Navy craved.

Keeping your posts messages focused and short will be a very good benefit for you and for your listeners (to notice you and inter- act with you) as they know you better.

ACTION: Craft 3 posts (using the KISS principle) that you would use to introduce yourself in your online network, ask friends or colleagues to vote which one describe you better, use the one that wins this mini-contest as your first post (but do not make this post alive it yet, just keep reading...)

13 ADD HASHTAGS

A hashtag is a label used on social media sites that makes it easier to find posts or information with a theme or contains specific content.

If you want people to easily find you on social media or even forums, using hashtags makes it easy to cut through online info clutter. However, you will need to use creatively to help to position your- self online.

I use it in two ways: One creating my own unique hashtags to reinforce my positioning or personal message.

e.g., #nowyouknow which became the title of this guide, is one example of a created hashtag as branding.

The second way I use hashtags is aiming to reach a particular target that helps you to get closer to your target, niche or listeners. e.g., #entrepreneurship if you are trying to reach startups founders or entrepreneurs.

There are many other ways to use hashtags (e.g., Tracking promotion's activity across many social platforms).

Whichever way you use hashtags, the main learning here is that you are better off adding the right set of hashtags into your posts (*Note: On Twitter a trending hashtag can boost your post views even if you do not have many followers and it can be an excellent way to gain traction on the platform*).

ACTION: Craft 10 creative hashtags that are unique for your positioning. Basically, 10 hashtags that represent who you are now, show them to your friends for validations and brainstorm if necessary.

14 YOU HAD ME AT HELLO

The online world is quickly get bogged down by info overload. There are literally millions and millions of posts, videos and marketing materials online right now.

Therefore, you must make people remember you and you need to make your message sticky, you need to make it unforgettable. Your posting or sharing must be memorable.

If it's not, then people will not remember you and your message and the chance they will ignore you is pretty high even if you apply the hashtags lessons on idea #13 or even everything we learned so far.

From the movie Jerry Maguire, most people remember two phrases: "Show me the money!" and "You had me at hello". I remember more than that because I already saw this movie over 20 times.

So, my point is you need to craft your own unforgettable phrases, the masterpiece of yourself.

It's your personal slogan or tagline and "have your listeners at hello".

ACTION: Craft 5 personal slogan or taglines. Try to put into words: Your character, skills, passions…It should be short and sweet and should say what you do and why you do it, e.g., "I am Batman: I conquer super villains and make the world a safer place". Show those 5 to your friends for validations and brainstorm if necessary.

15 TRANSPARENCY & PRIVACY

Your listeners will like it if you are transparent (show your heart or open up to them) They will feel connected with you. But you must limit how much information you put online.

Transparency can go very right or go very wrong. Transparency should not be the final goal. It is more like a commitment to share true information online.

Remember, be always true to yourself and your listeners, but confidentiality is a good thing to remember too, don't overshare online.

You don't have to let people know what year or where you were born, which could make you an easier target for identity theft online. You also better off limiting information about your family or whereabouts.

Unfortunately, we now live in a world where everything you share online will be registered into someone's mainframe somewhere.

Therefore, your job will be to strike the right balance between transparency (about yourself and/or personal message) and keep your privacy untouchable.

ACTION: Go back to the posts you have already done and perform a privacy check, is there too much personal information being shared? Are there ways to rewrite the posts without giving up about your privacy? Find that right balance.

16 ALWAYS STAY UPDATED

Your posts should always be fresh and new. One way to keep up with that is to make sure you are aware of current events or trends.

Stay updated, so you are not left behind by others online, at the end of this guide, there is a list of resources (references) that can help you with this hard task to keep up with the latest news.

You need to check for current events but you need to focus more on news that involves your positioning, niche or targeting.

You can also make posts about these news events if you do not side with any group or adopt other voices/tones that is not your own.

Remember, always credibility comes first, then speed.

If you get that right, your listeners will see you as a reference on what's happening online or offline, the person to go to when they want to know what's happening around.

ACTION: Craft 3 posts (just as practicing) about a big global event happening right now (The pandemic as I write this line), about some news in your professional field (a new innovation or breakthrough?), about some news in your local city or state. The idea is to see how faster you can craft a reliable and unbiased post based on some current event or breaking news.

17 THE UNIQUENESS RULE

Idea #14 talks about how you need to make your post or sharing memorable to your listeners.

Uniqueness here means you need to try going out of your comfort zones sometimes. Think of new exciting ways to make your posts so your listeners are not bored.

Looking for unique content idea for your posts?

There are lots of resources online that can serve as a base for you to craft your own unique content (again check reference page on the end of this guide) but overall, the unique rule should include: Visually pleasing things with your personality DNA stamp on it and be crafted in a way to generate a two-way communication (reciprocal way via comments)

The truth is sometimes a unique content in one corner of the online world can be a common place in another corner, and that can be played in your favor.

I give you an example I use occasionally, I grab a content trending on Twitter, put a twist on it (add my own words/description, for example) and place it on LinkedIn where usually things move slower than twitter.

So, the content may appear fresh and unique on LinkedIn, but it is not so much on Twitter anymore.

ACTION: Craft 3 posts complete out of your comfort zone but applying the uniqueness rule (should be visually pleasing, has your personality DNA and generate a two-way communication with your listeners)

18 HUMOR IS VITAL

Professionalism should be observed at all times, but some humor will put a smile on the face of your listeners. If they are entertained, they are more likely to coming back for more. I use that tactic all the time.

Share a funny or interesting story from your life but be natural. Never force humor out of you; it does not work that way. A laugh should be earned and not enforced.

If you are not a funny person is ok too. Humor is not only about jokes. You can be a very good observer and have the natural ability to dig fun out of everyday life.

A psychology researcher named Rod Martin created the Humor Styles Questionnaire, the first scientifically validated measure of humor.

The HSQ divides humor into four main styles:

"Affiliative, Self-Enhancing, Aggressive, and Self-Defeating. Affiliative humor means cracking jokes, engaging in banter, and otherwise using humor to make others like us. Self-enhancing humor is an optimistic, coping humor, characterized by the ability to laugh at yourself or at the absurdity of a situation and feel better as a result. Aggressive humor is characterized by sarcasm, teasing, criticism, and ridicule. Self-defeating humor is attempting to get others to like us by putting ourselves down".

ACTION: Take the Humor Styles Questionnaire to find more about your individual sense of humor. Please visit: https://www.thecut.com/article/whats-your-humor-style.html and answer the 32 questions on the bottom of the page.

19 SAY NO TO MEDIOCRITY

The quality of your online content you create / upload / share will have a huge impact on how you will be perceived online (personal branding or even your company's services or products reputation).

Build the highest standard for yourself. You must aim for excellence, do not settle for mediocrity.

Ask yourself: Do I have the best quality image (that support on what I am trying to express via my content), Did my text is well writ- ten (Or do I need to rethink a phrase or two), is the video the best resolution I can get it and so on…

There are many ways to achieve excellence: You can benchmark yourself against the best, work very hard, learn from others, trial and error, don't be afraid to try other approaches, etc.

Whatever you achieve just make sure it is your best.

Striving for excellence is the proper state for humans, evolutionarily and biologically. You thrive when you strive, and you wither when you become complacent.

ACTION: Review all the posts you've created so far and try to improve them, perhaps rethinking a phrase or getting a better resolution image/video, this final evaluation (before posting) is key because you're building your standard level and should be aiming to reach the highest possible level.

20 CROSS PROMOTE

You are getting online, but there is a world offline too.

So, you need to cross-promote between those two worlds.

Let people know about your plans to go online or to join a particular online outlet before you actually do it, that may create some buzz and build expectations about your online presence even before you post. If you are already online, the same holds true "cross promoting between online and offline is crucial".

There are many simple ways to do that:

Introducing yourself (not spamming) on all online sites that you comment across the web, adding signature texts when you send e-mails, etc. Yet, do not forget the offline world, too, creating a business card with your online presence URLs is a good idea. This gives those who meet you offline the chance to check out and follow up with you online too.

Remember, there are a good number of people who spend their time more online than offline and vice-versa, therefore, you must target both and cross-promote.

ACTION: Create some offline materials that support your online presence (imagine you are attending a conference or event with like-minded people) So, a business card is a must but not the only thing, you can create a small portfolio of your work or a 30 secs elevator pitch about yourself based on your online profile tagline… Create those materials now.

21 "FOLLOW ME" IS DEAD

Two things you can never do online, one is spamming, the other is to beg for followers / like and/or attention.

Like I wrote before, the name of the game is not to build a gigantic number of followers or be loved by everyone, you want to build a few good listeners that will carry your message online (and probably offline as well).

When you beg "please follow me," "please like me," you are showing to the world you care more about you than others. Plus, you are probably attracting only bots and/or people who could not care less about you and your message / content.

The "follow me" might have worked before, but today is pathetic. You don't shout "Marry Me" to every single person you see on the street, right? I hope not.

People will follow you if you do your homework (all the actions on this guide) and create outstanding content, help others online and just give time to time.

You should be building a natural relationship online (just like offline), and for that, you cannot beg for it or hurry up, it should be happening naturally.

ACTION: Create some CTA (call-to-action, more on that later) phrases to add in the end of your posts without sounding you are begging for followers or likes (Be open about your goals, be honest and direct. E.g., "I need someone to laugh about my weird mind, are you in? No, mommy not you…")

22 JOIN NICHE GROUPS

Get connected with other groups online which are related to your market niche and offer a match with your personality and goals.

For example, do you want to be an aircraft pilot? Well, better join a group that covers the subject and offer a network of pilots or do you want to be an entrepreneur instead? Same suggestion, find where entrepreneurs hang out online and join them.

By becoming affiliates of other online groups related to your field, you are exposing your virtual presence to more potential viewers and hopefully, future listeners.

Benefits of joining such niche groups include:

You can easily find topics relevant to your niche, ideas for future postings, seek help and support (especially important when moving to who you want to be) and as a big plus, it will be much easier to find out what your listeners (and members of a particular niche) love or have in common, when you know that, you just need to craft posts that trigger these positive feelings.

ACTION: Do some research on online forums, internet communities, social media groups, message boards... And initially choose 5 niche groups that are a great fit for who you are now and choose 5 niche groups that are a great fit for who you want to be (future). Keep expanding over time the number of those groups, do not settle for only 10 groups.

23 ORGANIC GROWTH

Organic growth is the process by which a company expands on its own capacity. The same process can successfully grow your presence online.

I am a big fan of natural and steady organic growth online and offline.

In the past, I was pretty worried about getting a viral post, I was constantly checking how many people look at my profile, how many people liked my post, how many "followers" I got it … Then, I realized that worrying about all those metrics is the opposite of adapting an organic growth.

Just like in Music, some artists come and go in a flash, got one hit and boom disappear forever, others stay longer in the entertainment industry even if they do not make a hit album every year.

So, organic growth will test your patience and will be more manageable in the long run as it is a less stressful way of being online. All of your growth should be done manually, organically, and without any fake followers, or software/bots, more on that next.

ACTION: Remember the metrics you have created on Idea #2 on this guide, review those (metrics) and align them considering the organic growth path, for example, if you had some milestone that would require you to be online 24/7 to achieve it, cross that one out and adapt your metrics to the organic growth strategy.

24 NOT BUYING FOLLOWERS

The good thing to allow you to slowly grow your presence online is that you avoid mistakes I actually did when I was beginning online.

One day, I had this "brilliant idea" to buy followers on Twitter to speed up growth (that was around 2013, so long time ago), I purchased those fake 10K followers because I thought it would attract many real followers if they noticed my followers increasing. Fast-forwarding to today, I see this as a good lesson, my followers did not increase because of the follower's counter but because of my content that got improved as time passed and resonate more and more with some followers that later became my "listeners".

So, take my advice and quit on pursuing followers, again you want "listeners" even if it is your brother, mom and daddy today, organically it will grow, trust me and yourself.

It will save you also money and a headache, if you buy followers nowadays, it will be expensive and may even get you banned on some online networks. Again, you are aiming for building a relationship online and turn viewers into listeners in the organic and natural way, capiche?

ACTION: Go and buy 1,000,000 followers, no problem, I wait… (just put this here to see if you are skipping the reading and just doing the actions :) Just kidding, no action needed here this time, just take a break and make sure you have completed all the previous actions up to now. Next will be working on your checking routine.

CREATING SOME CHECKING ROUTINES

"The problem with quotes on the Internet is that it is hard to verify their authenticity."

~ Abraham Lincoln (source: the online world)

25 A CHECK-ACT ROUTINE

Here is the thing: The online world is time-consuming.

It's up to us to decide how we will use our time. We can use it properly or waste it. Therefore, you will need to setup some kind of a check-act routine plan (for every time when you go online) to keep you focused. Otherwise, you will spend most of your offline free time lost on the online world. Is that a bad thing or a good thing? It depends and I am not here to judge but to guide.

So, let's establish a social media check routine, for example: once a day or 4 in 4 hours. Just so you do not become a slave of the net, take it easier, you are doing a marathon (organic growth) and not a 100 meters' sprint race.

Checking twice daily may be is all that your online presence needs initially. If so, there is no need to spend all your offline breaks performing a check several times a day.

That will vary from person to person and it is up to you to craft that check-act routine and see what works best for you eventually.

ACTION: Go ahead and write down how often will you be checking your online interactions and what will you do during this checking time slot. So, include on this check routine all the duties you will be implementing on that time slot (e.g., reply a comment, check on what is trending, connect/follow a new person, join a group, post something new, and so on …)

26 CHECK FACT MISTAKES

If you are following this guide order, at this point, you just finished your draft plan of the contents ideas and decided on your check-act routine but posted nothing yet.

Therefore, let's continue on checking act road and expand on this subject

Don't trust the internet at 100%, what I mean here is that many people lose their credibility very easy by just sharing something they saw or received in seconds, but they do so without spending a valuable extra time on double-checking the veracity of the info.

It just takes a minute or so to just google the subject yourself and see if that rings true or not, check what others said about it and make your mind if it is worth to post it or not. That's also true for your own contents you are creating, double-check everything.

As time goes by, you will get better on spotting doubtable contents on the online world.

This rings even more true, if you hired people to find contents for you or make the videos or graphics, it will be necessary that you check it for errors first before you share it online.

ACTION: Go back to all your posts ideas you have created so far and triple check for credibility (quotes, facts, affirmations, when it happens, where, trustworthiness …) This is crucial for building your credibility online.

27 SPELLING & GRAMMAR

Have you heard of the "Grammar Police" online?

The "Grammar Police" are those who seek to have correct English written online. They will correct bad Grammar and Spelling, and flame the user who posted that, sometimes ridiculing the post itself just because of one or two grammar or spelling mistake.

So, you want to avoid them, especially at this phase you are trying to build a credible image. Grammatical errors and typos can tarnish your image.

People will think that your posts are done in a hurry with no regard for quality. If you take, for example: Twitter, what matters the most, is that you say what you want in as few words as possible. If it can be deciphered, grammatical errors are encouraged. As a result, spelling and grammar on Twitter suffers terribly and that might be acceptable on Twitter, but the problem is: People are bringing these habits into their everyday lives.

Therefore, creating some kind of checklist that involves spelling & grammar before you post anything is a good idea.

ACTION: Create a checklist for spelling & grammar (including check for: misspelled word, verb conjugations, homonyms (words that sound alike but are spelled differently) proper grammar and punctuation, etc.). Also go back to all your posts ideas you have created so far and check them all with the checklist you just created, before the "Grammar Police" knock on your online door.

28 FINAL THINGS TO CHECK

So, what we are doing here is creating a good checklist that will help you develop a habit (first consciously by following each item on the checklist and then unconsciously as you get used to do this check over and over again) these series of checkpoints will be important in the long run so making them a routine from the beginning is a must.

However, a couple of things must also be checked:

For example: Test the link you are posting or sharing, you can easily do that by copying it into another tab and double-checking if that is working fine or not. When you're copying and pasting, it's easy to copy and paste the wrong one or leave off the last character, so checking is always prudent.

Double-check the image or videos in two ways: (1st) When you're using an image or video from elsewhere, wherever possible, give attribution through a tag or a mention (if you know who's the original creator).

Not only is it the kind thing to do, but it can help boost your credibility. (2nd) Check if the image/video is previewing correct before you click the post button. Preview is very important for people to click on it. Sometimes, I replace videos just because the preview screen was not that appealing.

ACTION: Add those two points (test link and video/image preview checks) into your final checklists created from ideas #26 and #27. The idea is to have a solid checklist that will prevent errors and avoid you looking silly.

LET THE POSTING BEGINS...

"The journey to grab a thousand listeners begins with one interesting post."

Flavio "Lao Tzu" Souza

29 A CATCHY TITLE

The world online is busy and chaotic; How do you get people to read what you write? It takes more than good content or great design. The most important part of writing a post or article is the headline.

Often, people online will not even try to read your post if they see that a post is overlong. So your job is to incite their interest by starting your post with a catchy and captivating title. If a title is something inappropriate to have, for example, in a tweet, then simply start the sentence with a catchy and interesting first sentence.

A catchy title or headline should come from you and not be a formula (remember idea #11: One voice and one tone) however, consider some points:

(1) It takes time (sometimes over an hour) to come up with a good catchy title, (2) you can use what, why, how, or when as trigger words (e.g., "How to cut your own hair") (3) Use emotional adjectives (e.g., absolute, unbelievable) (4) Your own created hashtags, I actually use this a lot (e.g., #NowYouKnow, #Meanwhileintheparalleluniverse).

You might end up with something like: #NowYouKnow: How You Can Effortlessly Cut Your Own Hair

---

ACTION: Create a catchy title to all the posts you've created so far (That might take a while, so focus on this task before continue on reading this guide, it's important you craft a memorable title/headline without giving out the rest of the post, remember the goal is to make your listeners read the whole post and not only the title.

30 GO FOR RELATIONSHIPS

Your goal online should be about building relationships, establish reputation (preferable as a helper initially) and gain trust from your listeners and the online community.

However, a catchy title or a post content should always reflect this core goal.

You should not be online to do a quick sale or take on a cold-blooded opportunity that shows up. Be building relationships. Your initial posts should reflect that: "I am here to help, not to take". Remember: You are in for the long run.

I am writing this here because I do not want you to misunderstand that a catchy title means to deceive your listeners and make them read your post or click on your link (clickbait). That's not what it is.

Reputations are built with content; Relationships are maintained with favors or help from your side. People want to know that you are an honorable, and trustworthy human being.

Use a mix of Mother Mary Teresa and Vito Corleone (from the movie The Godfather) approaches. Madre Teresa is your kind side that just give away (80% rule, remember?) and Don Corleone is your side that says hey I needed a favor back, can you help me here now (20% rule).

ACTION: Post an introduction post about yourself (using the Mother Mary Teresa approach) "You're here to help". Let the Don Corleone approach for later (on part 2 of this guide).

31 DO "SIGNATURE POSTS"

What are "signature posts"? They are posts that people can recognize you, your voice, your ton, your style. People might identify that the post came from you.

In writing, this identifying people from their writing style even has a name: It's called "stylometry", and it's based on the analysis of things like word choice, sentence structure, syntax and punctuation. In one experiment, researchers identified 80% of users with a 5,000-word writing sample.

To craft this unique perception on your listener's mind via constant "signature posts" will require time and creativity. But the sooner you develop your unique "signature posts", the better.

Your unique observations and life experiences will develop your individual writing stylishness and subsequently your "signature posts".

It may take a while to nail down what your style is, but if you are committed to being heard online, you'll have to carve out your own unique posts.

ACTION: Check if all the posts you have done so far has something in common, can you classify them by theme? Or do they have a word that seems to appear more often. Your task is to create a link between all your posts, create an identity unique to yourself, in order word: "Signature Posts".

32 AVOID POLEMIC TOPICS

Avoid posting (included sharing media contents) which are potentially offensive to any group or people.

Racism is especially a sensitive topic nowadays. Avoid commenting, even a slight joke, because people are not likely to take it lightly.

The list goes on and on: Abortion, death penalty, religion, gender differences, political views, etc.

Remember, you are trying to build a credible image and such topics can work negatively toward this goal (so avoid it at least on this initial phase).

As you gain more listeners and start some private discussions online, you can add your opinion about those subjects (listed as polemic topics above) later on.

While you want to avoid negative, non-productive related topics, it's good to post on topics that can inspire positive debates on important issues. Act more like a moderator and avoid taking sides on those constructive topics.

ACTION: Make sure you have no polemic topics (included videos / images) on your posts developed so far. Then work on creating 5 posts that would inspire positive debates in our current global affairs. Do that without direct expressing an opinion about those topics but encouraging a beneficial discussion over the subjects.

33 NOT BRAGGING BUT …

Do not just tell stories about others or a successful customer and/or client. Instead, update your listeners with your own achievements.

Not bragging but informing your listeners about it. This kind of posting is a lot more personal and convincing than keep only sharing a random texts or videos.

This is one of the benefits of making such announcements often. Your listeners will feel they are not left out of the latest about yourself, and they will feel connected with you and that helps to build relationships in the long run (more on that in the end of this guide revised edition).

The key here is to be humble on those updates, but if you won a Nobel prize or an Oscar, then you can go a little bit over the top, otherwise keep it modest.

Some social outlets even have their own expression for such "bragging approaches", for example, in Instagram:

"Insta-bragging" is a contemporary phenomenon. Tagging exotic locales, famous people, and showing off an expensive lifestyle, is inappropriate in the eyes of many who cannot afford such luxury.

ACTION: Create an announcement post about a recent achievement or a future one close to come into reality (e.g., like graduations or completion of a course), remember to keep the focus on humbling informing and not on bragging about it.

34 NOT ONLY ABOUT YOU

Do not always just talk about yourself or company.

Shout-Outs express greeting or praise given to someone in the presence of many people. Just like in the offline world, shoutouts improve team spirit. Therefore, do shootouts or talk about your listeners too.

Their achievements should be equally important to you so share it too.

If you speak about your listeners, they will feel they are noteworthy and that they also can count on you to spread the good news around. This will improve your relationship with them.

So, your job is to pay attention to announcements by your listeners. If something is going on in their life, acknowledge it.

It boosts confidence and gives your listeners a sense of pride. Who doesn't like when someone notices how hard they have been working or to hear that they are inspiring someone.

ACTION: Check your listeners' profiles and pick up two recently accomplishes or announcements they might have posted and give it a re-share or/and an authentic comment.

35 LISTENERS COUNTER

When you go online, one of the most outstanding metrics that most people measure your success is by the number of people "following" you, like I wrote before that should NOT be our ultimate goal. However, because of that obsession with this metric worldwide, we can use this in our advantage.

It is advisable to update your listeners about increase in subscribers/followers.

Usually, people update about their first 1000, 5000, 10,000 and 100,000 subscribers. Make these updates so your listeners can see that your online presence or reach is moving forward. Again, not bragging about it but informing and thanking them.

Some social outlets even have special unlock features for your account when you reach certain levels, and paid opportunities are within your grasp when you reach such levels.

Whatever you do, here is something you should never do: Add the numbers of your followers into your title or profile's tagline or description. That's a no-no because you give the wrong impression that you are online to just collect followers and not building listeners. Plus, there is always a bigger fish, you add something like this on your tagline: NAME and 50K followers, how that will it look like for someone who has already 1M followers?

ACTION: Craft a post every time you reach a milestone update on your subscribers/followers counting giving emphasis on thanks not on the numbers/counting.

36 ALWAYS ADD VALUE

Adding value should be the core of your posts, you can share knowledge and personal success stories to your listeners and anything you want, but make sure that every single post or share you make has some kind of learning or gain (for your listeners) on it.

Remember, Mother Mary Teresa approach:

Give, give, give …

My "foodforthoughts" (yes, in the plural) posts / hashtags try to add value by showing different views or opinions about a subject or a problem.

But there are many other approaches to add knowledge, wisdom or just be inspirational to your listeners.

You can do how-to-do approaches if you are good in DIY tasks, you can take a photo or take a screenshot lesson from a book and share it (go ahead choose one lesson from this guide, I do not mind), you can also share a free resource (e.g., an e-book) or some info or link you happened to find online and you think that would benefit some of your listeners.

Whatever you do, do with your heart and not with self-marketing intentions.

ACTION: Craft 5 posts that touches on the approaches listed above (DIY, book lesson screenshot, free e-book, free seminar...)

37 ALWAYS BE COURTEOUS

It is a mistake to think that your behavior online should differ from your offline one.

The online world misleads individuals to think that they can hide behind masks of "anonymity" and create different personas online. The "stealthy vile" persona that some people assume is a growing threat for adolescences, specifically when it originates cyberbullying.

The world offline as well as online needs good and courteous people. So, do your part.

On days when you have nothing to say, maybe a simple "Good morning" and "Good evening" or "Happy week ahead" will do. You may also use greetings as an opening to an announcement post or to share a personal opinion.

Your listeners will continuously enjoy a courteous attitude and a courteous person always attract another courteous person, so it is a win-win in the long run as well.

Our online behavior should mirror our own inner image.

Therefore, be kind, positive and polite to everyone around you offline as well as online. GoHumans!

ACTION: Create five original empathy statements that are personal and unique to you. AVOID crafting the "customer service plain vanilla approach": "Welcome to [INSERT COMPANY NAME] Customer Service. My name is [INSERT NAME]. How can I help you?

38 TALK ABOUT TRENDS

Talking about trends show you are updated with the latest tendencies. That helps to build the image you are the guy to go when a topic requires the newest views or opinions.

Because I run a site dedicated to technology trends and innovations to talk about trends in the techie field is an easy task for me.

So, if there is a particular field you are very connected with professionally or you are passionate about it, let's say fashion or music or any other, why not to craft posts showing the latest tendencies on these areas.

You can use visual resources (like graphics or charts) to help you to develop your thoughts in a simpler and clearly to explain those trends.

It's important to make your observations "jargon-free" and keep your explanations very unpretentious so everyone can understand without knowing the field terminologies.

ACTION: Create 5 trend posts close to your heart. Something you know well or care about it. Don't forget to add visual to make it self-explainable and pretty easy to understand by an amateur, use those graphic resources in your favor to back up your thoughts and assumptions too.

39 AVOIDING COPING

Coping and paste is a dangerous game online, you are trying to build your unique online presence and want to be perceived as an authentic and one-off individual.

Therefore, copying someone's post or comment is never recommended. It's pretty easy to get a catch with a simple visit to google search.

However, sometimes, sharing a similar picture or video will happen when two or more people come to the same thought or encounter the same material or source of inspiration.

That is ok as long as you keep your tone and voice (write your own take from the subject). Like a DJ, you can remix it.

In other words, let's say you are surfing on the net and found this amazing post online, don't copy and paste it, try to reflect on the subject and put your own spin on it.

Rewrite the post in your own tone and voice.

ACTION: Find 5 posts online that you think it is great, rewrite them using your own words, tone and inner voice. Can you find a new way or approach that the original writer missed? Can you make it shorter? Can you make it simpler? Can you expand it?

INTERACTIONS...

"Don't argue with people online.

Every classroom had a kid that ate paste. That's probably who you're arguing with."

Anonymous

40 THE "HATERS" TRAP

There are many good people online, but there are also "bad apples" ("The haters").

The truth is those "haters" don't deserve one nanosecond of your precious attention, so why would you give them any? Just don't! They will steal your time and mood if you get into their trap, which basically consist of teasing you to respond by leaving direct hateful comments on your posts or publishing nonsense public judgements about you.

Again, "haters" seek a reaction from those being hated upon. Never give them one, as your mission is to build listeners and not haters, when you encounter such revolting people online, I suggest you just delete the comment and block the person without second thoughts (more on that later) and move on.

The problem isn't the aversion being thrown at you, the problem is when people react to the "haters" that starts a snowball of negativity which is not good for anyone online or offline.

If you add the fact that some of those "haters" can be even a bot or machine (in other words, not even real persons) Why would you ever want to get into a discussion with them? Answer: You don't.

ACTION: Got a hater comment on your post? Take a long, deep calming breath for 40 secs and close your eyes and picture yourself calm. Press delete/block and move on.

41 DON'T DELETE, REPLY

Ok, when I said delete the "haters" comments, I was not referring to use this action on every comment you don't like. It's not that, there are comments that is negative, but it is fair, can be someone who has a different opinion than yours (and that's ok), can be someone that is pointing out one mistake you did or a point you missed (also ok).

They are not "haters", although sometimes they might lack a bit of "kindness spice" on their replies or comments.

So, what you do is up to you, you can leave it unanswered (more on that later) or you can try to reply in a very polite way, just to let the person know that you read their comment, but at the same time, avoiding to give the person a reason to start a chain of negative replies or discussions. You can say something vague like:

"Thank you for your comment, although, I do not fully agree, I take your point". Now, that's much more civilized than the bitter comment with no reply and curse he/she for 5 generations to come…?

If the person still keeps their aggressive approach after that by making a second harsh comment or giving a dry reply than you might be facing a hater, if so, just stop the interactions, delete the comment/block and move on.

ACTION: Work on a couple of plain vanilla (but polite) replies you can use when you face such a situation online. Remember to keep it short (a phrase or two).

42 REMEMBER VOICE & TONE

The interactions are when your voice and tone should shine. If you are a nice person, usually how you handle online interactions will say millions about you. So, do it well and do it in an honest way:

If you are an introverted person, reply as an introvert, if you are open person, do the same. You are trying to be the closest possible of your real self when interacting online, no sweet, just be yourself.

Remember, people value honest interactions offline as well as online. It's like that famous law of attraction book, you are a good person, you attract good people, you are a happy person, you attract happy people and so on. No need to adapt your inner voice or tone to accommodate others.

The right listeners for you, will come to you as long as you keep it real without faking personalities.

The truth is if you want to interact successfully online, then you must create a friendly and truthfully online persona. To do that, you start by handling your manner carefully so it adds an aura of expertise, compassion, and professionalism to your persona. Besides that, always make your listeners feel welcomed, inspired, and appreciated.

ACTION: Craft a couple of replies (for future use) that makes your listeners feel welcomed (to drop more replies / comments), inspired (to visit you, for more) and appreciated (there is something for them to gain from you).

43 NEGATIVE COMMENTS

We already touch on negative comments on idea #41, I would like to expand a bit on the idea on how to turn around an initial negative comment to something positive.

Some people believe that the first impression is everything, so on that 5 secs that a person scan you from head to toe (if you are meeting offline) or reads your profile or gaze your profile picture you supposed to be perfect.

Well, sorry to break that idea up, but that is a superficial thought. Sure, you can get an initial idea about a person (usually empathy), but to really judge a person, you need to give her/him more than 5 secs. That is when interactions play a big role online.

So, the best way to turn around negative comments into something positive is to basically be super nice and polite, that's the secret, very simple. So, someone left a negative comment, give him/her a second chance and write a positive reply. He did it again (negative), do once more a positive reply. You can set a number for the cut-off, I usually set on 3, it means if a person leaves 3 negative comments in the same post (including their replies), I just move on and stop answering or replying.

ACTION: Set your cut off rule (how many chances will you give a person to amendment their negative attitude toward you) Give a thought also on what kind of replies, you can craft a "standard reply" to use repeatedly (for new people commenting, not your regular listeners) or do case by case replies (more indicated to regular listeners).

44 LEAVING UNANSWERED

Know which communications should be left unanswered. You do not need to respond to every question or comment.

As the number of your listeners grow, it will be harder and harder to keep up answering all the questions that will come in your direction.

You need to read all of the questions (to judge them and be fair with everyone dropping messages or questions), however, answering those will be up to you.

A question can tell a lot about a person, does the question is well made, is it relevant to the subject or to you? is that on your interests or expertise? Isn't the answer of the question already available on the post?

(e.g., The title of the post might say: "From Japan" and then on the comment area someone is asking, where is this from? Crazy, right? Yeah, but it happens a lot).

Most of the time, those questions or message will also be a general sales pitch probably being sent out on bulk, so if you cannot help the person out or there is nothing there for you, just leave it unanswered.

ACTION: Work in a simple checklist to see if a question or a comment pass your own judgement and deserves to be answered or not. For example: You can define if the question is about religion (or any other personal topic), you will not answer it and so on, create this checklist.

45 USER'S ARGUMENTS

Sometimes, the dispute may not be between you and a user but amongst users themselves. If so, do not lose time to act and intervene.

The idea is to remove these as soon as possible. I usually give one chance for the users to come to peace with each other and stop quarreling (I basically remind the users that kind of behavior is not appreciated by the other users (included myself)) and if that does not stop the clash, then I step in and remove the user's arguments (deleting them) and block the users if necessary.

Sounds a bit of a "censorship" but you have to think of your listeners' constructive mind, your job is to keep the harmony between your listeners and always work with them to optimistically keep the discussions with a tolerate tone and mutual respect.

You have to take the best decisions in pro of the majority harmony among your listeners and if two people arguing and fighting are not fitting in, you just let them go and move on. Like I wrote before, your job is not to make everyone your listener but focus on the ones that resonate with your inner self.

ACTION: Continue the work you have started on action 44 and expand that checklist to when two or more users are furious exchanging insults. Would you give them a chance or two to fix things up? Or do you remove them right the way, what kind of discussions is not tolerated?

46 HEATED CONVERSATIONS

Sometimes, the conversation starts nice and everything is going ok with mutual respect and well-mannered exchanges of opinions, but out of the blue, everything goes ballistic.

Leave the now heated conversation because it is dragging your energy up, but you do not want to be perceived as abandon the conversation or even worst "silence consenting" a point or two made by the person that switched to the heated mode.

So, what do you do? Well, there are many ways to graciously step back from a heated conversation.

The most common one is to buy time (or tomorrow is another day approach) you can say something like: "Let me think about that." Or You can also consider "You may be right" Or "I understand" (Remember: Understanding doesn't mean you agree).

It's up to you how you will handle heated conversations but usually angry online discussions keep you spinning in circles and usually make the problem worse. Do yourself a favor, avoid heated conversations at all cost.

ACTION: Build a list of swear words to have in hand when the heated conversations start, just kidding, build the opposite, a list of diplomatically phrases you can use in heated conversations. Creating that in advance when you are in calm and relax is a much better tactic than do it alive.

47 POLEMIC SUBJECTS

At this stage, you are in the part 1 of this guide or you are building your present image, creating your honesty credibility online.

So, at this crucial stage polemic subjects are better left out.

We already talked about avoiding polemic topics on idea #32, in order to avoid any possible misinterpretation of your thoughts and confuse your initial listeners. Remember, at this stage, you are online to help out and not cast doubts or judgements.

As you progress (time and to part 2 of this guide) you will see that as your listeners are getting build, they will appreciate your opinion about polemic subjects. When you talk about those polemic subjects online just remember biased language (or "political correctness" in vogue nowadays).

It frequently occurs with gender, but can also offend groups of people based on sexual orientation, ethnicity, political interest, or race. For example, you do not want to accept common stereotypes such as "blonde women" or "smart men". How you exchange opinions with your listeners, what assumptions you make or beliefs you assume about it are choices you make as an author of posts and sharing, so keep an eye on choices.

ACTION: For the time being, just avoid it. As you feel comfortable to get into those subjects later on, then just speak your heart and be sensitive to other views or opinions.

48 WHEN MISTAKES HAPPEN

Ok, Mr. Always right! You just made a big mistake online, yes, you, so what comes next?

Delete the tweets in hope anyone saw it, is a risk move because depending how famous you are, everyone gets that screenshot that later on get viral on the internet with your mistake you said never happened.

So, the best approach is the simpler one: My bad! You shout to the whole corners of the online world, follow by a sincere apology.

Even with a lot of precaution you learned from your checking routines exercises, it is very possible that a mistake or two could slip up.

When this happens, just admit it and apologize. Your listeners will appreciate this better, if you do not do it, they will see you in denial and will hate you for that.

Expect all the "haters" to show up when mistakes happen, do not sweat. If you apologized, you will be fine.

I have experienced some cases where "haters" continue to remind the world about my mistake over and over (after I apologize), However, because I have such a wonderful group of listeners, those listeners jump in and put the "haters" back in their places. So, be always thinking on what is the best for your listeners.

ACTION: There are more than one way to say "I am sorry", can you think of five more? Write it down then.

49 QUALITY CONVERSATIONS

That's your goal when it comes to conversations and interactions online. You want to build quality interactions among your listeners. The idea is that those conversations or interactions have to have a deeper meaning and proposal for you and for them, if correctly done, it will flourish into a beautiful friendship. So your job is to kick off that kind of value conversations.

I usually use the hashtag GoHumans! on subjects that shows positive individual examples of our human kindness. That can spark worth conversations that helps people to restore their faith in humanity and that is a great outcome.

So, whatever your online goal is, you have to direct the conversations to that objective without pushing nor forcing it. How do you do that? By pointing people into different perceptions or new ways that help them to think differently about a subject. You can also start quality conversations by simply touching on what you and your listener have in common, this is known as the similarity-attraction effect.

Whatever you do, you should implement a "philosophy of quality" on your conversations, that's why it is important to start any conversation with that in mind. However, to keep that quality going is everyone's responsibility.

ACTION: Think of interesting conversation topics that complement your online goal. Those topics should correlate with your passion or at least be topics you are knowledgeable enough to talk about it.

50 BE CONFIDENT

As time passes, you will naturally become even more confident. But the truth is: The path to be confident is in your hands.

To go over this building process of more confidence online, you follow what we have done so far.

Avoid controversial topics, stay away from anger arguments or empty discussions and apologize when you make a mistake.

As you adapt those rules and stick with the subjects that you are good at (or at least did a good research about it) You will be just fine. Just relax and be yourself.

While some people appear naturally confident with themselves, most of us are not. Luckily, self-confidence can be developed and will grow in time.

What triggers your fears? What makes you feel anxious? Why do you not trust yourself?

Once you figure out everything that makes you nervous, you can build on the areas where you need improvement and gradually change. You only feel insecure and self-doubting if you're not prepared.

ACTION: Repeat after me 10 times: "I can do this!", Now seriously, be always prepared and stop worrying and developing negative thoughts. Be confident is key.

Plan 2.0:
MOVING FROM WHO YOU ARE NOW TO WHO YOU WANT TO BE

"To infinity and beyond!"

Buzz Lightyear

51 THE UNCONSCIOUS MIND

According to Freud's psychoanalytic theory of personality, the unconscious mind is a reservoir of feelings, thoughts, urges, and memories outside of our conscious awareness. It is also the part most influenced by suggestion and imagination.

A suggestion that seems to strengthen ideas already present usually produces action.

So, in part one of this guide you were targeting your listener's conscious mind (Because you were new to them and your listeners were fully consciously judging you to see if you can be trustable)

Now, it's time to target your listener's unconscious mind, remember you are trying to make a change from who you are now to who you want to be in the future. To be done in a sublime way and WITHOUT DECEIVING tricks.

Let me give you a simple example: you are not thinking about your smartphone, but now that I mentioned you probably want to check it. So, the unconscious mind comprises mental processes inaccessible to consciousness but that influence judgments, feelings, or behavior (actions).

ACTION: Your task will be to find out what your listeners love and make posts that trigger positive emotions on them. Read also this article: McLeod, S. A. (2023 updated). Unconscious mind. Simply Psychology. https://www.simplypsychology.org/unconscious-mind.html

52 LISTENER'S TARGETING

Do you already have a well-defined vision of who your target market niche is? The next thing you need to figure out is how you can appeal to them.

You need to go deeper on the research of the idea #4 (study your target), this time you should research on the things that interest them (your market niche/listeners).

For example, if you are a specialist (or have services /products) in the cosmetics space and your target market niche are women that use makeup, then perhaps some video content about maquillage tricks will resonate with them. It's not a one fits all approach, because your listeners will vary in so many ways, from having different tastes to diverse interests.

Therefore, creating some kind of basic classification to aggregate your listeners under "one roof" is an interesting approach to narrow down the target, it calls segmentation in marketing.

The easiest way to do it is to classify (segment) your listeners by demography: Geographic location, gender, age, race and so on.

ACTION: Classify your listeners in segments, identify them (your listeners) and aggrupation. See if you can pinpoint something in common between the different segments you created. The key here is to find a trace of what your listeners might have in common (e.g., can be something simple as geographic location).

53 EXPANDING ONLINE

Now, joining groups inside of one platform (e.g., Joining groups on LinkedIn or create lists on Twitter) is good, but it is too restricted.

You'd better out expanding your presence online beyond social media platforms; Don't put all your eggs in one basket (in this case, one specific site).

The online world is always changing, five years ago nobody outside of China knew about TikTok (Douyin in China) and now this platform is popular worldwide. Imagine if you were one of the first in your country to build a solid presence there, you would probably be a star on this outlet by now.

So, you need to keep an eye on what's happening online and looking for interesting new platforms in line with your goals and who you want to become, joining those platforms in an early stage, would give you some sort of "first move advantage" and that pays off when the platform become mature on your country or world- wide.

Nowadays, social media is a great place to help you get exposure online but it is not the only one, you can expand online via writing a blog, developing apps, starting a website, making your own video content, podcast … So, my point is you do not need to limit yourself to social outlets, there is much more to explore and grow.

ACTION: Join another social media channel to expand your online presence or/and start something on your own (like a blog, podcast, vlog…)

54 HIRE FREELANCERS

As you already noticed, being online and developing your charisma is a very time-consuming task.

If you really intend to become successful online, you must outsource some tasks, otherwise you will become a "binary prisoner". Study shows we're already spending an insane amount of time online (as users) and I cannot advocate for you to spend even more developing your presence online.

Therefore, a freelancer or assistant is a must.

The most important key in hiring any freelancer is knowing PRECISELY what you need and what they can do/provide.

For example, I am not an expert on SEO so I subcontract this part to a freelancer. So, you need to identify those tasks where you are not excited or interested to work on, or something that you don't have the skillset for and then outsource it.

It will not only free some valuable time from you but also the deliverables might be way better than if you did all by yourself.

ACTION: Check the resource page (in the end of this guide (WRITING TOOLS section) and go to Fiverr using the link address there because you will get 20% OFF in your first buy) Do a search on the offers and professionals over there and bookmark the ones not from your area of expertise or a complement to your skills (e.g., SEO, Marketing Promotions, App Developers, Designers…)

55 STUDY WHAT WORKED

Now just because we moved to who you want to be (future) phase, it doesn't mean you need to reinvent the wheel.

I'm sure many posts you have done worked well and perhaps some did not. You need to perform an analysis and study what worked for you and what is working for others.

Let's look on your past posts, which one drove the most interactions, check if they have anything in common (e.g., A particular voice and tone? or went out on a specific time (e.g., evenings or morning), was it new and fresh or a repost? And so on)

This is analysis will shed lights on what worked, then you can try to replicate that approach once again to experiment if it will work again or not.

You can also expand this analyze to other users of viral posts (most shared and commented posts), we can always learn about the features of viral content from others and use those steps to improve our own content.

ACTION: Create an excel file for your 10 best posts so far (or the latest 10 if you cannot identify the best 10), then analyze them and try to find a pattern (commonality), check things like: Text length, post title or headline, subject, context, voice and tone (was it emotional or controversial or reserved?) what was there for your listeners (solved a problem, taught something new, motivated, had humor…)

56 RECYCLE A CONTENT

Sometimes, you just run out of a fresh new content. While recycling contents is not something you want to do often, occasionally, it is the only thing that could save you. But if you must perform this, make it look new and distinctive enough from your past content.

It's also important to double-check if the recycle content still holds true when you post, social behaviors keep changing fast these days, which may be the case that a post worked before (let's say 6 months ago) but today would be classified as an "offend post "or not appropriated due to some particular event.

The recycle content that works better are photos that may gain a new caption or can be collages that allow you to use a collection of images to tell a story or showcase points. (Before and after approach)

You can also recycle contents from offline to online, use E-books excerpts written by you for posts, and vice-versa.

You can also republish a guest post you did some time ago on someone's website to your own blog. The golden rule here is to recycle YOUR contents (the ones you wrote), not someone else.

ACTION: Going back to the action #55 where you created an excel file for your 10 best posts, try to rewrite those 10 posts with a fresh perspective or a new approach. Keep those 10 posts on standby for when you reach a creativity block along of your online journey.

57 LEARN FROM FLOPS

Also, on Idea 55 we checked what worked, but you can learn a lot from what did not work for you or others.

Nowadays, celebs aren't the only ones who get tarnished press for posting inappropriate and sometimes downright offensive posts online against their better judgment, any regular Joe (like me) can get the same treatment for infantile faults.

As one example of such a silly mistake, don't ever talk trash about your employer online. A frustrating day or experience is not a good reason to broadcast online your complaints with your employer. This behavior is not only inappropriate but also can easily get caught these days, again even if you think you deleted a tweet, someone could have taken a screenshot and that can easily go viral.

My point here is that you can double learn from flops in two ways: Via other people's mistakes and avoiding it to replicate those failures and from yourself. Even sharing someone else's post can get into trouble online and that is why we talked about avoiding polemic subjects on idea #47.

ACTION: Focus on your mistakes so far (even if it was minimum) see what went wrong on your post, is there a post you missed the tone or tried to use a different voice that was not your own, for example: You tried to be sarcastic and it backfired (it'd have worked if you were in a comedy club) Check those posts and remember them (to avoid repeating the same mistakes), study and learn from them.

58 INCREASE THE VOLUME

As we are trying to move from where you are now to where you "want to be position", it's time to increase the volume.

What I mean by that is that it is time to bring your online presence to another level. Increasing the volume here means: Post/Share more.

If you were posting three times a week, time to double that. If you were doing a post a day, double that or even triple it. It's important that your listeners notice you are now stepping up your efforts (being more active and interacting more than before with them).

One benefit of increasing the volume is that your posts will stretch to different time zones and reach new potential listeners and that is favorable to help your online growth.

I recommend you take the slowly and healthier "increase the volume" path, which means moving in your own pace and without compromising your post qualities and lose your voice and tone.

ACTION: Plan the increase the volume act in advance and at your own speed (when will you increase the volume and by which consistency), work on the post development and create a buffer of at least 10 posts before posting more, plan that in advance, so you keep a constancy and do not run out of ideas so fast. You can start simply doubling your post and when you feel comfortable gradually increase the frequency.

59 A HIGHER STANDARD

You will need not only increase the volume; but also you must increase your standard. You must aim to a higher standard. If your posts or interactions with your listeners were good, now it needs to be great, you need to be a collector of "Wows" from your listeners.

And that will only come when you keep improving your standard. For example, see how any YouTuber improves their quality over time, check their first video and the latest one for comparison, most of the time, you can clearly see an improvement of their standards (from visual improvement to better presentation skills).

One easier way to improve anything is to make it more customizable for your listeners/audiences. Perhaps, it is time to focus on a particular subject you have been collecting positive feedback. Perhaps you could develop further your own personal branding. There is always a way to do it better and you should not set for a particular standard but keep always improving.

We talked about adding hashtags (idea #13), can you improve that? Make those hashtags even more memorable? Think always on ways you can improve your posts and your presence online.

ACTION: This is one straightforward action, imagine if you could go back in time and improve your posts, what would you change or make it better? So, from now on use those improvements you thought out, going forward.

60 FIND WAYS TO CASH IN

When I said you should increase the volume (idea #58) and you have to find a higher standard (idea #59) that means you will be spending a lot more time online.

So, you must cash in online otherwise, your time will be spent with no financial benefits and that is not a good position to be. So, how can you generate revenue online, I will expand on that later but here are 3 initial ideas, you can implement today:

Sell ads (sponsored contents), Sell products (physical or digital ones), Sell services (promote your services or skills) And often, you can easily do all three.

So, let's quickly review those 3 possibilities:

If you have built many listeners and your interactions are happening, why not considering cash in on your efforts? You can offer "sponsored contents", you do not need to be an "influencer" or have "millions of followers" to do that, you can do it right now *(Check Fiverr on the resources part of this guide, you could offer a sponsored contents GIG over there)*, the same goes to sell products and services, consider doing an e-book specific for your listeners and audience or let them know what you can do (remember 80%-20% rule (idea #8), so it's time to pitch more your 20%.

ACTION: Go to Fiverr.com and spend time analyzing other people services, can you create a GIG based on your own skills (e.g., translation, programming, social media promotions…) If so, actually create GIGs there.

61 EXPAND OFFLINE

Although we are spending more and more time online, there is a jungle out there called "the offline world" so, you should not lose sight out of it (even as Covid-19 looms).

What you are trying to build here is a strong online presence, but the bypass product is you create also your "personal brand" or "a signature". Therefore, expand offline as there is a good crowd looking for ideas and solutions offline too.

Ok, so what can I do to expand offline (you might be wondering) Well, you can start offline communities that meet occasionally or create local events that helps to expand the interaction among your listeners and yourself.

But not only that, you can expand to areas like: Entrepreneurship. For example, you are an expert on pairing wine with food, well you could do offline events, courses or even rent restaurants for a short period and offer "signature menus" for your listeners.

In today's world, offline engagement generates a lasting stamp that stays with someone beyond those brief online interactions. The truth is you never forget the people or brands who made a touchable difference in your life.

ACTION: Review your goals (Idea #1) and see if you can pin down 5 ideas to expand offline, e.g., can you create a workshop event around "who you want to be"? can you create a local club around your area that would meet once in a month? Give thought on expanding offline.

62 BUILD YOUR ONLINE SPOT

Now in the same way, you should be expanding offline (idea #61) you need to cut your dependence on outlets you do not have control. We can see how dependence on social media can be very risky, YouTube, Twitter, Facebook … They can easily ban anyone from their networks if they want to.

So, if you are hard building (spending countless hours on it) your online presence, you can NOT be dependent of such social media outlets, you need to have your own spot where you can be sure all of your efforts will not go to the drain because of a tweet that Twitter's CEO does not agree on it.

By creating your own website or community channel is how to go and it pays off in the medium/long run.

The benefits of doing that are enormous, you can control the interactions with your listeners, you can be more open to share your ideas (and your listeners too) and overall, you can have a better financial return too.

As today, you better draw a plan that incorporates the physical (idea #61) and claim your own spot in the digital world. Your final goal should be: Turning online listeners into real offline acquaintances.

ACTION: Look into easy ways to build websites (if you do not have one yet, e.g., check WordPress) and develop a plan with measurable milestones to slowly drive your listeners from your current online spot (e.g., social media) to your own online home/outlet.

63 BRAND YOURSELF

You probably have built some brand around your name or profile by now. But why should you be branding yourself even further is because it helps attract the right listeners.

Optimizing your online presence to convert new visitors into listeners is the move you must do and your branding will play a crucial role here.

Let's start with a simple question: Is your current username adapting "The KISS principle" (idea #12) in other word, is it simple, memorable and easy to find online?

According to researchers, it takes less than two-tenths of a second for someone browsing online to form an impression of your profile or bio. So, from username to profile/bio it needs to be telling a unique story: A story about you.

You need to describe who you are, what you do, and the story behind your skills or products/services and finally how you can add value to your listeners (what's in it for them). Your brand should reflect yourself (voice and tone idea # 11) and be true (do not risk your credibility by lying) and be built so it helps to attract the right potential listeners.

ACTION: Time to rebrand yourself to who you want to be, do not be afraid to reinvent yourself from the bottom up, don't be afraid to use both text and emoji (https://www.piliapp.com/twitter-symbols/) to save space on your message.

POST PART 2

"A person is a fool to become a writer. His only compensation is absolute freedom"

Roald Dahl

64 GO BOLDER

As you are noticing to move from where you are to where you want to be, you have to step up your efforts and that means that your interactions will also go bolder.

What I mean with bolder here is that you slowly can open up more to your listeners and let your opinions and knowledge flow out more often, you are still avoiding polemic topics (idea #32) but you can let your opinion be heard more often.

Be aware that the bolder you go; You may lose listeners along the way. That's fine, because you are being true to your convictions and beliefs, so those listeners were not mean to be for you in the first place.

So, as a practical example, your posts can expand into other topics that perhaps you were not covering before or you can add a line or two about why you think posting or sharing a particular post adds value to someone.

The goal of being bolder is to show you are true to your brand and that you are focused and determinate to create a new positioning for you (clear showing you are moving away from who you are today to your new you (who you want to be in the future).

ACTION: Review idea #7 (Planning your contents) and do it again the same action #7 but this time focusing on who you want to be positioning and going way bolder than before with the 2 weeks' advance of posting ideas.

65 MAKE PREDICTIONS

Nobody wants to predict anything in this crazy world we live in (especially in 2023), but if we are getting bolder, we need to take some calculated risks such as going to prediction posts.

Now, you need not dress up as a future teller and stare into a glass ball, to do that nor to get 100% right all the time. But you need to do some research of trends in your area (or the area you are moving to) and write those predictions about where you think the "puck is going to be" with a good level of conviction.

If most predictions come true sometime later, that will be very helpful to solidify your online presence/brand and that is very beneficial to attract attention and opportunities.

Forecasting the future is very in vogue these days, companies are hiring "data scientists" and anyway that is good in decrying patterns. Like I said, you will need to have done good research over the subject you are trying to make a prediction for it. You also must know that predictions can be two types: Linear: When you have a start point as reference: e.g., Predicting how things will evolve from 2023 (your start point) to 2050. The other way is what I call "teleport predictions" without a clear start point. e.g., Predict the year 3501…, usually, this last type of prediction is the hardest to get correct (without a DeLorean time machine)

ACTION: Craft 3 post predictions after research about the theme you choose, remember to be related to your goals and new positioning of how you want to be perceived in the future.

Sneak peek posts can work in two ways: The first way is that helps you not to waste days (or weeks) waiting your post or story to be perfect.

Although you need to keep your high standard (idea #59) sometimes, it is better to give your listeners a sneak peek (or bits) on what you are working on it even if everything is not finalized yet. Therefore, anticipation of an announcement or a new product is a great tactic to use with your listeners.

The second way is that can also help you to collect initial feedback, I use sneak peek posts to ask for feedback /opinions from my listeners, I use this approach particular with logos and slogans I am developing (giving them a preview) and ask for their feedback (e.g., which one they liked it more, you can do that in a poll too, we will talk about that later).

Sneak peek posts can also be a great tool to bring your listeners to a "call of action", for example, to subscribe your newsletter (in a way to build your own online spot idea #62) more on building newsletter later.

ACTION: Go back to your most successful post so far (pick the best 3 that got the most engagements), do a training exercise to see if you can break those 3 posts in bits of information, make like a story with chapters or transform them into sneak peek posts.

67 AND THE WINNER IS...

Hold a giveaway: This can be as simple as asking your listener to comment to enter. If you are doing sweepstakes as company, then you better check the laws on your country before do it.

Sweepstakes is where the winners are chosen by the luck of the draw, there might be some requirements to run such draws.

Prizes can be almost anything you can think of from handmade goods to an all-expenses-paid trip.

You can also run contests that choose a winner based on some merit. The winner is chosen based on some criteria such as best comment, funniest story or tip, etc.

The most complicated form of giveaway is a lottery where people must pay money to buy a chance to win. Lotteries are highly regulated and should not be run without consulting with legal counsel.

Anyway, the important point here is to hold a giveaway to interact and reward your listeners (more on that later).

ACTION: Pretty simple action exercise here, just work on creating a giveaway (think about the rules, the goals you want to achieve by doing so, the prize, the promotion timeline, the call of action, ROI, etc.).

68. A POST SERIES

I do this on LinkedIn occasionally, share a series of similar posts over a certain number of days or when a post is too big to share as one, I do a series and divide it in parts.

e.g., #NowYouKnow: How to use an iPad like a Pro 1/3

Then later I continue in another post: #NowYouKnow: How to use an iPad like a Pro 2/3 and finally the last part: #NowYouKnow: How to use an iPad like a Pro 3/3

Announcing the series with an introductory post can also be a good idea. And here is why first it let your readers know what is coming next (it creates some sort of anticipation) and make you liable to finish what you've started or promised.

Especially, if you have created your own blog There's nothing like telling your readers that you'll be writing a post series around a certain topic to keep you inspired and accountable for the assignment (that's what I did with this guide and now I am delivering it).

ACTION: Do a brainstorm and create a post series around a theme you know well or you want to be perceived as an expert (moving to where you want to be in the future approach). It's important to craft also an Introductory post (generally an announcement about your coming up post series), the posts do not need to be long posts, but it needs to be well researched if the theme is new to you. Remember you do not want to do a post series where your data is outdated or your facts are wrong.

69 GIVE EVEN MORE THANKS

A simple thank you can go a long way to building connections with your listeners.

I am not saying you will "incarnate" Oprah Winfrey (It's a meme called: Oprah giveaway, "you get a car, everyone gets a car") and say: "You get a thanks, you get a thanks, everyone gets a thanks".

As we discussed on Idea #58 (Increase the volume), you need to also increase your interactions and a thank you more often to your listeners can make miracles. However, sometimes a simple "thank you" can lose its value if repeated over and over.

How to fix that? Well, you need to go a bit deeper than just a simple "thank you" and translate that meaning in actually action, for example, you go to one of your listeners' profile and read his/her last post or article and give your feedback and thoughts. So, the idea is not a plain vanilla "thank you" but a "thank you" with a payback.

E.g., "Thank you for sharing my post, I paid a visit to your profile and enjoyed what you wrote (name of the post), when you said (specific post/article phrase) resonated a lot with me, keep rocking!" You just need to be more meaningful than a simple "thanks".

ACTION: Create an excel file where you list your listeners (username) and rank them per interactions, one interaction equal one point, the idea here is to pinpoint who are your best listeners and keep tracking on that. Then, say "thanks" to the top 10 and repeat that often.

70 RECOMMEND LISTENERS

Recommend your listeners to other listeners, in other word, encourage the interactions among themselves on your network: Share their posts to someone else's that would benefit from it, mention their profile and encourage your listeners to directly interact more with each other.

By recommending others and their posts, sharing their "tweets" and thoughts, and engaging them in a conversation online, you are bound to get a ton of good karma back and that will also benefit your own online growth.

Nowadays, it is pretty common on social media sites to have suggestions of similar profiles that someone might also want to check out, such as mutual friends or other people they might know.

Recommendation online works just the same as offline, you basically advocate other people you believe is worth your listeners to know or at least to check it out their profiles or their projects.

It's important that you know and trust your listeners very much first (and that will come with time and interactions) and then promote them, never do the other way around.

ACTION: Based on the excel file you created on Action #69, pickup your best 5 listeners so far and recommend their profiles to other people in your network. Repeat this action occasionally, the more you give, the more you receive, that is how the universe works.

71 POLL QUESTIONS

Studies show that people usually like answering quick poll questions online. The problem is users misuse this function and saturate their listeners with poll questions too often.

You have to try doing poll questions sometimes to entertain your listeners or break the ice. But keep it related to your positioning and use it to gather feedback about your posts or how can you improve going forward.

Polls questions let you know the preferences of your listeners. This will show you how to better define your next goals or plans (Idea #1).

You need to be creative here as people will be turn off if your poll questions are too obvious (everyone already know the answers), too specific or narrow (something only someone with specific knowledge could answer) or too irrelevant to your listeners (e.g., let's say you have a specific target group of listeners (teenagers) and your poll questions are about how house mortgage fees will behavior in 2 years from now).

Use poll questions wisely and remember to always share back the results with your listeners, that will motivate them to participate.

ACTION: Create a poll question (you can choose a general feedback on how are you doing on your posts/articles or ask some particular question related to the file to know more (remember the goal: To move to "who would you want to be")

Everybody loves the memory trip posts; I have even created a very specific hashtag just for that kind of posts (#meanwhileintheparalleluniverse).

My idea is that sharing something from the past (e.g., your childhood best toy) can be a great way to create a bond with some of your listeners with the same toy as favorite too.

As Ferris Bueller (fiction character played by Matthew Broderick in the movie: Ferris Bueller's Day Off) well said: *"Life moves pretty fast. If you don't stop and look around once in a while, you could miss it."* Your goal is to remind your network of such gems.

Therefore, without being too nostalgic or sounding too melancholy, you can use the memory trip tactics to create that special "generation" bond with your listeners.

Just like the previous idea (#71 Poll Questions) just do not overdo it, because you might have listeners that will not get the references and be annoyed with those posts.

Anything that evocates certain memory (from objects to places) can be used here as a memory trip post.

ACTION: Craft a couple of memory trip posts. The secret is to choose something that has been famous in the past (e.g., when you were younger), but somehow it is in the limbo these days. Those work the best for that WOW moment "Hey, I remember that!".

73 RANDOM TIPS

Periodically post a random tip to your listeners would be something that they can find useful. You can use a random tip number to adds interest to your post (e.g., Tip #436: *"Laughing is good for the heart and can increase blood flow by 20 percent"*).

You can target those random tips to a particular subject or theme or just make it wilder and natural (as comes to your mind).

There is no rule to follow here, just make sure your tips add value to your listeners and it is positive.

Keep also those random tips true to your voice and tone, plus do check the veracity of the tip.

For example, a quick search on Google confirmed the above statement: Laughing is INDEED good for the heart and can increase blood flow, the percentage of increasing will vary though, but it seems at least by 20 percent is a reasonable statement to say.

So, double-checking (Idea #26) is always a great move.

ACTION: Search for some random tips online, and pick up about 10 tips you could use as a post when you run out of ideas on what to post, decide on what to pick and what to pass, remember to align with your voice and tone. In the end of this guide, you can see random tips I placed there, you can craft something similar too.

Do you have any hobbies? How long have you been doing them? How did you get started? What common misconceptions do people have about your hobby?

Hobbies posts can also be an excellent ice-breaker and can generate great interactions.

Again, you are trying to increase the volume (Idea #58) so you need to think about new posts so you do not get bored or mechanic on doing your posts. Remember, always aim to higher standards (Idea #59).

Hobbies are a good theme because it is personal, but (depending on your hobbies, for example, I am a vinyl records collector) still protect your privacy (I just share LP covers or songs).

Another advantage of sharing hobbies online is that you attract people that share the same hobby, plus your listeners will be pleased to hear that you are interested in getting to know them in a personal level and share a common hobby.

Still, making friends online can be hard, and takes time but if you both already share something in common, it might be a bit easier and faster.

ACTION: Do 3 posts about your hobby or hobbies (or if you do not have one, something that sparks interest on you), the overall idea is to open up a bit in a personal level with your listeners via those posts.

75 BEHIND-THE-SCENES

It's behind-the-scenes (BTS) content and it works great for companies, but on the individual level, you can have the same benefit:

It builds trust, sparks relationships and grows deep connections with your listeners.

One way you can use BTS content is to share progress and success (Idea #33). Got a new book coming up? Share the cover ideas for instant feedback, got recognized somewhere on what you do, show the BTS on getting this recognition.

As you can see from this last example, BTS contents do not mean showing only a prêt-à-porter event behind the scenes, but you can show your listener how you get there.

As you know, I am a big advocate of funny contents online, and I am not alone on that, according to BuzzSumo, funny content ranked in the top three kinds of posts that provoked an emotional connection with people.

So, if you have a BTS funny moment (involving you (the poster, and NOT about other people having a hard time), share it. You can use BTS content to show your human side (yes, I make mistakes too).

ACTION: Brainstorm on how you can transform some of your successful contents so far in a BTS type of content. Do you have some old pictures that show or illustrate your story, or shows your progress or what you went through, if it is also funny you might have a BTS content winner here.

Ask me anything is an idea that usually are used online in two approaches:

When people are drunk or under the influence of alcohol (Never ever do that, post something online in such state, just forget about that)

When a person is famous and goes online revealing their identity (Of course, because the online world is full of people impersonating someone, always double-check on that before kickoff interactions)

So, the way I recommend you to use the "Ask Me Anything" approach is to basically announcing that you have free time online and you would accept questions / interactions from your listeners so they can know more about you. That's it, that's the correct way to use it.

Of course, you are not obligated to answer all the questions (especially those that touch on your privacy issues) but when that is the case, just be polite and refused to answer the particular question and move on.

It's important to always keep comfortable on doing such content, if you feel that the questions are not going to the right direction, you can also fix a topic (e.g., Ask me anything about marketing and so on).

ACTION: Craft 5 topics you know well and you are comfortable to be challenged online. Post them when you have free time (e.g., end of the day) or do limited time you will be answering questions (e.g., In the next 1h).

77 SELF-QUOTES

Self-quotes are one of my favorite content's creations (although I rarely do it), the thing is the online world is full of people quoting someone and I always wondered if they (themselves) could not come up with their own quotes.

So, developing your own quotes, it is a nice move and sharing that will help your personal branding and positioning online. Your quotes should be 100% authentic (really coming from you and not stolen from someone else) and very important: Be creative please.

Self-quotes may come to you naturally and most probably when you are not online, if so, keep collecting those raw thoughts through the day (write down so you do not forget it) and lapidate those "raw thoughts" later and extract into a simple quote.

You can even create some visual to go along with your quote, like we saw on idea #9 (Not only text) sometimes a picture or a photo has much more impact than only write down a simple quote and share it online.

You do not need to be perfect when you drop a self-quote but because your name will be tag alone with the quote, know what you are saying or claiming.

ACTION: Because self-quotes are very personal, I will not ask you to create a certain number of quotes, just for this action/exercise, just keep self-quotes alive on the back of your mind and when you stumbled upon a thought (or a learning situation) that you could make into a self-quote, just do it.

Most people miss with this idea, usually people love to tag "influencers", "celebrities" or heavy users but without a content or questions relevant to them.

That shows two things, they are doing so just to crab attention from those users and they did not study or prepare well their approach. Do better than that, to tag famous people you need to make relevant to them and to you.

You can tag them in a question you know that they are experts in the subject or they would be pleased to share their opinion/view on it. That's why you need to do a research before you tag on someone.

I am no celebrity and I receive a high volume of tags (people tagging me in their posts) it's hard to answer every tag, so do not take it personal if the person you tagged on, did not answer you back. Because humans are very curious creatures, I bet even if the "influencer" did not answer, he or she probably read your question (or at least their staff did, in case of celebrities).

It's ok, keep trying different approaches (do not need to be only questions, you could share an article or a news that might relate to someone you are tagging along).

ACTION: Identify some users ("influencers", celebrities or heavy users) that would make sense to your "who you want to be in the future" strategy, study their profile, try to understand what (content/ info/questions /interests) would make them to go wow if you tagged them.

79 NO AUTO-POSTS

Forget about auto posts (Remember Idea #59 (higher standards) not quantity but quality)

Auto-posts are like plastic in the ocean, nobody likes and it is very easy to spot on, they float (just like plastics) and it does not have your ton or voice (with auto-posts).

I know auto-posts save time, but it is soulless (we will talk about scheduling posts next which is different). What I mean by auto-posts is those random posts generated by computers or bots and they usually are posted just to keep your activity up online (during nighttime, for example).

Even if it sounds a good idea to automate your presence online (and there are some tools for that, check the references in the end of this guide), auto posts are definitely not the way.

Auto-feeding your blog or site updates are also a no-no. You have constructed a unique voice and tone online so far and you need to keep and protect it. Do not risk by "outsourcing" your content creation to a bot or HAL 9000 (the fictional artificial intelligence character and the main antagonist in Arthur C. Clarke's Space Odyssey series)

Do never lose control over your posts/feeds in pro of gain of speed or time, it is just not worth the tradeoff.

ACTION: Straight forward action here: Just forget about auto- posts that are not created by you (respecting your tone and voice) but robots or online bots.

Now, to schedule a post (crafted by you) to be published at a later time is a good idea and will help you to enhance your online presence in different time zones.

Sometimes you want to specificity a particular time for publishing (e.g., Let's suppose that you discovered the majority of your listener's prime time would be around 4 am in your local time (due to time zones differences between you and them) so schedule posts tools will help you a lot on that kind of situation).

Such a tool that will help you schedule a post, will alleviate you in the morning (and bring down your stress level to have to wake up so early day-after-day).

Another benefit is whenever you take a break (or a vacation), but do not want your listeners to wait until you return from the retreat for news or updates from you.

As you can see, definitely the usage of scheduling posts has clear benefits and should be on your radar when you face a similar situation as described above.

ACTION: Do some research on scheduling web tools or software (e.g., Some social media outlets like Instagram and Twitter have particular tools that work better for those specific platforms than others that might work better for blogs or website, for example. So, you need to spend some time researching which tools will work for your particular case. Again, in the resources section in the end of the Now You Know guide might help you too.

81 TOP LISTS POST

You can use top list posts in two approaches:

To let your listeners know what they have missed during a specific period (e.g., Here are top five stories you may have missed during the week.)

As personal ranking and reviews (e.g., Here are my top five films of all time.) We all look for reviews or opinions before buying or consuming something, so an insight in ranking is always welcome.

Top list post works well because it drives interactions and sometimes even hot debates, just remember (idea #46 heated conversations) to control the course of those discussions if they go too wild.

Be creative on crafting top lists posts and even more importantly, make it relevant to you. Make a connection: For example, instead of saying: Top 5 books in 2023 (which everyone might already know), try something like Top 5 books (that I read and fully recommend) in 2023. Now, it connects with you.

Lastly, top list posts that shows off your professional knowledge or skills (without being too overconfident) are also a good idea as it gives credibility to you if they are well done. Those need to be very accurate in order to not backfire.

ACTION: Choose between approach 1 or 2 and write down 3 top lists posts using your creativity. Make sure it connects with you and your goals (especially, related to who you want to be in the future).

82 NEWSLETTERS

Like we talked on Idea #62 (Building your own online spot), collecting email addresses from your listeners is key if you want to nurture a life-long listener's community. But it is not always an easy task as you will find few folks willing to share their information without good reason.

The problem of newsletters as collector of info is that sometime people make the mistake to ask too much (fill out a newsletter form, with name, address, company, for example), you need to focus in one data only: Your visitors or listeners email, that's it. You can always follow up later and ask all the other info (as long you have the email collected in the first place).

However, creating a newsletter is a must to do nowadays because it is how to start the immigration of listeners under one platform (that you probably do not own e.g., Instagram) to your own (or future one) that you will give you control, direct access to your listeners and increase in value of yourself as creator of content. A lot of resources make creating a newsletter easy. Check "GOT TO EAT TOO" BONUS TOOLS on the resources section in the end of this guidebook for the Mailchimp example.

ACTION: Think on how you will collect your listener's e-mails, developing a newsletter is just the first step, what kind of "carrot" (e.g., A free eBook?) What are you going to use to attract new listeners and make them give you their emails?

83 REAL TIME CONTENT

Everyone has some kind of morning routine, just like I do. You perhaps browse the online world for news and find the latest trends. So, why not make your morning routine into a real time content post?

For example, find a few of the most recent events in your industry and write about them. You can even link to news articles if you feel it is appropriate.

News is always happening, so you can always feed on that as a good source of ideas for your posts or just share for interactions. The important thing is that you add your voice and tone to it (opinions, analysis, etc.).

I use twitter as my "breaking news" app

(I especially check their trending now hashtags) to get a basic idea on what's happening globally around me.

You can also use the "real-time content idea" as inspiration for crafting an opinion post as you can read tweets with different judgements about a particular subject or situation just happening now.

The only key point here is freshness. A real-time content works like a "breaking news" idea on the traditional media. It should be happening/developing in real-time.

ACTION: Pay a visit to twitter (or a tradition news outlet, e.g., New York Times website) and pickup 3 of the freshest news you can find, see if you can give your own perspective or twist and rewrite that as a "real-time content" post type (Remember Idea #32 and avoid polemic topics).

A calculated risk is taken after careful reflection of risk probability, risk impact and returns. This can be contrasted with risks taken unknowingly or without much of an evaluation based on hopefulness or a lack of due diligence.

Therefore, you need to take the calculated ones, for example, if you are planning to start a new online shop or a podcast program that will require a certain amount of money, you must think in terms of if I fail do I go bankrupt? If so, do not do it, quantify the risks! And lastly, if it becomes a hit, what would be the rewards (ROI).

Now the same concept works for posting. At this stage you are "going bolder" (Idea #64) you can take more risk (calculated ones) in other to defeat your online competition.

I am advocating that polemic topics should be avoided but what if you have a different take on subjects like Politics, Religion, Society … Should you just be quiet about it? No, but just like walking among mines, you may do it if you want too. I sometimes post about politics or religion under the #foodforthoughts tag, what I do is to share a thought (sometimes an image) but without adding an explicit opinion about it. By making it loose on the topic, your listeners might appreciate it more.

ACTION: The action here is for you to create a framework of decision that will support your decisions in a calculated way. Remember (PIR): Probability (that will happen), Impact (if you do or do not) and Returns (ROI).

85 GO LIVE, SHOW YOUR FACE

Live streaming online has made the leap from uniqueness to essential. Social media outlets like Facebook, Instagram, LinkedIn and Twitter have integrated live video to their platforms and an increasing number of people and companies are adjusting their online presence respectively.

So, do not be afraid to show your face and jump to live streaming.

I did not do it yet, but I am moving in steps toward this approach and I recommend you to strongly consider it too.

There is no better way to create eye-catching content that improves your positioning in your listener's' mind as well as their news feed algorithms if you are using such social media outlets described above.

Live video feels bold. Very few things seem live these days, people are afraid to make mistakes and therefore avoid live streams, but if you do, it shows how real you are and that you're self-confident and willing to take calculated risks like this one.

ACTION: Think about all your contents you created so far, can you classify them per subject or themes, can you transform those classifications into a script or something along those lines that could help and guide you to talk in a live streaming for an hour or so? How about your positioning, are you comfortable to share your goals and ideas in a live show? Consider those possibilities and work on it for a near-future launch.

INTERACTION
PART 2

"If you want to change the way people respond to you, change the way you respond to people".

Timothy Leary

86 CREDIT YOUR LISTENERS

Got a good suggestion or hint from your listeners? Credit them.

If you've ever had someone take credit for your ideas at work, you already know how frustrating it is. So, how to go is to always credit and thanks your listeners (remember Idea #30, you are building a relationship with your listeners and trust is a must).

You can decide the best way to credit your listeners, you can do a mention (by adding a few words of thanks and then the credit to them) or you can indicate them as the initial source of your post (e.g., Via (Listener's name) Or as shared by (Listener's name)).

It's up to you on deciding which way works better for you, in crediting your listeners, the important action here is to give credit where credit is due.

Sometimes, it is hard to trace the origin of a post or idea on the internet. Therefore, when you cannot pinpoint the original source, better say something like "thanks for the sharing" instead of crediting someone you are not sure is the original person who posts that.

ACTION: Go ahead and practice crediting your listeners for ideas, suggestions or valuable shares. Like I wrote, there is no formula on how to do it but make the crediting action a habit going forward.

87 REWARD YOUR LISTENERS

What could be better than crediting your listeners? Well, how about to reward them? Go ahead: Offering discounts, luck drawing (Idea #67) or access to exclusive deals can be a good reward to those listeners that always interact with you online.

People love freebies and you don't have to give away a trip to Hawaii. The fact is, people don't care much on what they win but that they won.

However, don't reward someone with something with only value for you (the giver). I see many people online rewarding their listeners with their eBooks or their company's report. Honesty, and generally this is just a "cheap marketing promotion" and not a real reward to the "luck receiver" at all.

Rewarding people for participating, interacting, giving feedback, sharing ideas or suggestions and so on, require a plan and budget so you do not need to do it all the time. Another way to go is to do random acts of "kindness giveaway" occasionally (e.g., around a particular season: End of the year/ Christmas...) that works better as spontaneous acts and do not require pre-planning.

ACTION: Brainstorm on ways to reward your listeners, you can ask them to do a simple action (e.g., take a picture of your product or share something you wrote) to be eligible for the reward, for example, then think of a prize or something that adds value to them (your listeners), then decide on the date to run that.

88 A COMMENT = A "LIKE"

There's plenty of research that suggests social media usage actually triggers the release of dopamine (It is known as the feel-good neurotransmitter in your brain: It's a chemical that transmits information between neurons), thanks to dopamine effect every single share, like, comment, follow, etc…. causes you to experience a rush of positive feelings.

Plus, online interactions can actually increase bonding between individuals, as we view engagement as an act of human acknowledgement.

We're all people. It feels great to be appreciated and in the online world how you do that is with a "like".

A simple "like" works as acknowledge that you read the comment, liked what was written and as well as a "thanks" for taking the time to write one. So, it's a 3 and 1 package these days. A "like" can be very motivating and satisfying, and it builds relationships between you and your listeners.

So, every comment gets a like? Well, the ratio is not 100% because there are awful comments, spam … (remember the "haters and negative comments" Idea #40 and #43) but overall, I use it at 98% of the time.

ACTION: If you are not doing that yet, from now on, do it. Sometimes, your posts can go viral and you have hundreds of comments to check and like, that can drag some of your time online, but it's very worth to invest on doing so. A comment = A "like" that simple.

89 "HELP ME, HELP YOU"

Help others that are new online (or even if it is not the case), remember when you started online with little confidence and a bit on the dark on how to behavior or what to do. Well, it is payback time. You can help others online by sharing the knowledge you have.

It's true that people will forget what you wrote or post online, but they will never forget how you make them feel when they need some kind of help.

You can help in so many ways a new user or a listener, for example: Giving/sharing information about a topic you are knowledgeable or pointing them to the right direction to appropriate online resources (Wikipedia, Wikihow, Yahoo Answers, Quora, etc.) or a link, sometimes your help can be also useful if you know a particular skill (for example, if you know graphic designing) so you can help by doing a sketch or by giving a feedback over someone's work.

There are so many ways you can help people online all over the world. The best part of doing so is that it satisfies our mind and soul you are helping others.

In the end, "little drips of water are what makes an ocean" and we should always help each other as much as we can. GoHumans!

ACTION: Find a way to help someone online (your listener or not), might be a simple task for you but it may be the most valuable thing for the receiver.

90 A PROSPECTIVE LISTENER

How to spot a prospective listener? Well, I use this rule, if some- one comment on a post or an article I wrote, I usually reach back for inviting to connect.

Unfortunately, in the platform, I am in the most (LinkedIn), I have already reached their 30,000 max cap celling for accepting new connections so I can only accept someone new when someone else drops out (which happens occasionally, remember your job is to change "followers" to real "listeners", so when a follow drops out, it is my chance to add in a new listener.

You probably do not have such a limitation like I do, so invite any prospective listener you spot on. Look for traits or a pattern that indicates that he/she can be a good listener to have onboard, for example: Is the prospective listener a match to your tone and voice? Is he/she a group player? Is he/she polite? etc.…

Whatever you do, just do not go only for "titles or positions" as some criteria to add someone in, those are temporally and a bit short- sighted, although, there are exceptions (for example, invite someone that share a similar job position with you), the idea is to attract some- one that shares others things in common with you besides a title.

ACTION: If you haven't done yet, invite the prospective listener to direct connect or to join your newsletter. You have to tell them why and what is the value for them to do it so, do that by being polite and open about yourself. If a rejection of the invitation occurs, don't take it personally, just move on to the next prospective listener.

91 TAKE A BREAK

You are putting long hours of your life on this, sporadically, I recommend you to take a break of the online word.

Go for a "Digital Detox" and stay away from your digital devices for a period of time, I usually do that once in a year, but you do not need to follow the same schedule, you can do it more often if you want to.

I believe by taking a break, you can refresh your passion of being online and break a bit the addiction of being connected.

Transform that experience of not being online for a week, for example, into a post later on in other to incentivize your listeners do the same.

Let your listeners miss you when you are not around, most people take for granted your online commitment and they don't know what they've got 'til it's gone.

ACTION: Plan your "Digital Detox" (Digital detox refers to a period when a person voluntarily refrains from using digital devices such as smartphones, computers, and social media platforms), choose when to detox and for how long, craft and give advance notice to your listeners, put your electronic devices out of reach and have fun offline, you can share this Detox experience in a post when you return.

92 INDIVIDUALS REPLIES OK

Just because you are online, it does not mean that everything needs to be public and you cannot have one to one conversations via individual replies or chat and build friendship in this way.

Replying to people individually takes time, but it shows your extra consideration to your listeners and that is appreciated by most. Just make sure that when you interact with someone one-to-one (in privacy), you do it in the "P.R.S" (Professional, Respectful and Short) way.

Remember that nothing is 100% private online, so be careful what you write or advice online in the one-to-one way.

You can use this individual communication channels to understand and know a bit better about each of your listeners. Don't push for information, just let naturally happen the interchange of info flow/conversation.

If you need to say the same thing to a lot of different people, then a group message is how to go instead of reaching everyone individually. Keep big announcements as public messages so you avoid misunderstanding and unfairness among your listeners.

ACTION: Break the ice and take the initiative to reach out to your listeners individually. Perhaps, you can informally present what you are working on or share updates or info that might be interested for a particular individual. It's important you take the lead at this stage.

93 SALES PITCH INTERACTION

As we saw on Idea #60 (Find ways to cash in), you might be wondering if you can do "sales pitch interactions" with your listeners? Yes, you can but you need to be straight forward indicating that upfront, otherwise, you may lose their trust as they will be confused when interacting with a gain intent in mind and when you are not.

The other thing to notice is that those sales pitch interactions should not happen all the time, use here the same 80/20 post rule (Idea #8) where 80% of your interactions are giving always and 20% is asking something in return.

Perhaps, the most important here is regarding the approach/timing, you will need to be able to read the ambiance and know the best time to turn the conversation or comments replies into a sales pitch.

Timing and judgement are key, you don't want to jump the gun and give out a cold sales pitch when someone just asked you how are you doing or how's the weather on your side... Don't hurry up, again let things happen naturally and you probably do not need to even pitch. Your listeners will get interested on you and naturally ask what you do for living or how can they get your services professionally.

ACTION: Do some research on how others are pitching online (particular in your favorite social outlet). You will notice different approaches (direct, indirect), take note on the sales pitches that grab your attention and repro- duce them, adapting to your own voice and tone.

94 HOST ONLINE MEETINGS

If you have recently been directed to work from home due to the pandemic, odds are you're already familiar with Zoom. If not, Zoom is an application (similar to Skype) for remote work meetings online but that you can use to host any meeting online.

A meeting combines many ideas in one: It helps to drive quality conversations (Idea #49), helps "branding yourself" as expert (Idea #63) and can be a way to reward your listeners (Idea #87).

If you are already part of a niche group (Idea #22), hosting a meeting is an incredible opportunity to learn more about other members and share knowledge.

Collaborating on a presentation is made easier with Zoom's screen-sharing capabilities. The meeting host can enable multiple participants to share their screens. Even documents can be compared in real-time, presentations can be given with instant feedback and more.

Nowadays, because of the convenience of digital resources like Zoom and others, there is no excuse to not host a meeting online.

ACTION: If you are not familiar with digital tools like Zoom and Skype, spend time on getting used to them, then craft an agenda for the meeting (what's the goal? what's in for the participants?), send invites in advance… Most meetings are a failure before they even begin, because they lack of planning, if you are hosting one, think well in advance.

95 INPUT AND FEEDBACK

Don't be afraid to give your input and feedback to your listeners if they asked for. It's important to be honest, polite and constructive. It can be easier said than done.

When giving constructive criticism, it's vital to make sure you're presenting a balanced viewpoint, whether your feedback is eventually positive or negative. This is more noticeable when it comes to negative feedback.

Your input and feedbacks must be also effective. Effective feed- back is feedback heard, understood and accepted by the recipient.

Another good idea is to make your input somehow actionable. That means that the recipient should be able to change the action or behavior you are pointing out as problematic. You are guiding your listeners to a possible change and not giving empty feedback.

Lastly, feedbacks need to be clear and understandable by the receiver. Example of vague feedback: "You need to become a code-master". Example of clear feedback: To improve your coding skills, I suggest you read this book (book name) and keep tracking and documenting every single step; to achieve that, I recommend three things: …

ACTION: Because input and feedbacks must be asked for (and it is case by case), you do not need to prepare anything in advance, but be aware on what we have discussed here. If you are not comfortable (or proficient) to give constructive criticism, work on your feedback skills.

96 SPEAKING & INTERVIEWS

Don't forget to keep intermingling the offline world with your online one occasionally (Idea #61 Expand Offline).

Speaking at conferences and seminars, or being interviewed on a video show or podcast, can obviously be good for your personal branding, but they are also great ways to get exposed to new and potential listeners.

Best of all, people at meetings like that, are highly likely to relate to your plan of "MOVING FROM WHO YOU ARE NOW TO WHO YOU WANT TO BE", and they just got a good taste of your value, so they're highly motivated to trail you online for more.

Keep marketing yourself on both worlds (offline and online). For example, include your online footprint at the bottom of your presentation slide decks, as long as the conference allows it, and do networking after.

Overall, public speaking is a win-win activity that will support your expansions plans on the offline and online world, conference goers will travel far distances for the right speaker lineup and that will also give you the chance to meet people from different places and backgrounds.

ACTION: Write down 3 topics you are comfortable for speaking in public. From these 3 topics, pickup one closer to your heart and "sales pitch" yourself online for a conference gig (It does not need to be only speaking engagements, look into seminars that accept written research papers too).

97 CALL TO ACTION (CTA)

Although, you have defined your goals and objectives online a long time ago (Idea #1), you need to make sure that you are doing "calling to action" to fulfill those goals.

A call to action (CTA) is a statement designed to get an instantaneous response from your listeners.

The goal is to get your target market to respond by taking action. It's generally used at the end, or sometimes throughout a sales pitch (e.g., an ad) to let potential clients/customers know what to do next if they're interested in what you offer.

It seems obvious to have one, but some people forget to add one. Whatever you want your listeners to do: Sign up, register, call, subscribe, donate, buy order, share, download or click here ... You have to specific add a (CTA) in the end of your posts (not all the time but every now and then) otherwise, it will be harder to achieve your goals.

You can also add a "sense of urgency," which works because people have fear of missing something. For example: Offer expires on 24h, limited time offer, act now before supplies run out or enroll now to get early-bird price.

ACTION: Work on your CTA and prepare at least 4 types (A formal one, an informal one, a direct one (explicit asking) and indirect one (slightly suggesting). It must be short and to the point and **you need to** use your own tone and voice.

98 KEEP UP WITH CHANGES

Keeping up with new social media features and algorithm changes is a must, because usually when you get a better understanding on how things work (and don't work) online, it's when everything changes and you have to start over again the learning curve.

So, keep monitoring how the social outlet you are in (e.g., YouTube, Twitter, Instagram, LinkedIn…) is evolving. Do they announce some plan to add some feature? Or a change on privacy? Anything that affects you, needs to be a concern. The feed distribution algorithm on those platforms I mention above, can put all your efforts suddenly in a trash can with a simple change on the algorithm. The holy grail for those social outlets is to push you to buy/sign up for their advertisements/paid functions or to feed other posts that paid for ads to you.

If you don't control the feed distribution, no matter how brilliant is the post you wrote, it will go nowhere. So, you need to find ways to "hack" that limitations (this guide gives some hint on that). As an example: As today and by default, your LinkedIn feed is sorted by "Top Updates." These posts are populated based on the user's activity (think: accounts you regularly interact with via "Likes," shares and comments), so the more reactions you generate from your listeners, the more they will see your future posts.

ACTION: Study how the algorithms in your social outlet works today, so you can have a basic understand. Check for ways to bypass any "gatekeepers code" that blocks or slow down your efforts to reach your listeners.

99 GIVE TIME TO TIME

I am a believer of the organic growth path, as we talked on Idea #23, things need time to develop and bare fruits.

So, as we are reaching the end of this guide, you are probably thinking: Hey, where's my one billion listeners, hun?

Just like living organisms, your online presence will grow organically branches out at a rate that keeps pace with your own life. There's no Millennium Falcon in hyper-drive mode that will accelerate your online popularity in a day or two.

I am confident that you have all the resources and knowledge now to organically construct your positioning online and, more importantly, to arrive on where you want to be.

However, changing positioning (from who you are to where you want to be) is hard, but it is not impossible. It just takes time.

Understand that even if you did all the exercises here (And I really hope you did) it takes time to see its full effects.

So, as you all pursue new goals in life, I have two pieces of suggestion:

1. Pursue noble goals, not better results.

2. Be patient/Give time to time.

ACTION: Listen to Pink Floyd's song: Time.
Let the lyrics sink in.

100 HAVE FUN OR STOP

Whatever path you have gone online (Creating your own blog, a channel, website, participate on social media, podcast, vlog…), the important thing is to ALWAYS enjoy what you are doing.

As the rock band Queen wrote in Under Pressure: "If you feel pressure, pushing down on you, pressing down on you, no man asks for. Under pressure that burns a building down, splits a family in two, puts people on streets" … to be online, just stop!

Life is too short to spend staring at a monitor the whole day and getting nothing positive out of it. Your satisfaction comes first. The world is changed from within, not from outside. So, don't ever feel under pressure to a performance online, nor be harsh on you with the colossal task of "changing the outside world".

The idea #91 (Take a break) is there to help out a bit when your "plate is full" but it is not a permanent fix. If you feel it is not worth all the efforts and time spent online, just walk away.

You can still accomplish the same successful results concentrating on your offline world.

ACTION: Keep reviewing your goals and craft new ones, measuring not only ROT (Return Over your Time) but create some kind of happy index you can check sporadically, as we saw the online world can be cruel (Idea #40, 43 and 46), and your health and happiness come first. (e.g., I dropped Facebook because it was not making me happier)

101 **JUST BE YOURSELF**

Make certain YOU (or your company) truly represent yourself or your online positioning identifies you.

For instance, if one of your personal traits is positivisms, be positive online too.

In 2023, being authentic on social media is rare, most users seem afraid to show their real lives or their real way of thinking. Be authentic with your listeners, should be your number one priority. Don't change yourself just to resonate with your listeners.

I guarantee that your message will have much more impact if it comes from your heart, not from a planning thought.

So, just be yourself (according to a Zen book I read it means: *Follow your intuitions, become more aware of your surrounds and your thoughts, follow your bliss, and do what you love, you align with happiness and peace and that is what you are here for*).

ACTION: Smile, you are done. Congratulation on graduating from the Now You Know Guide Journey. Celebrate! Here goes my (CTA – Idea #97): Please take a picture of YOU holding the Now You Know Guidebook (if you are reading the e-book version, just take a picture holding your kindle or tablet device) and send it via e-mail to hello@flavio.online if it's ok with you, allow me to share your achievement with my listeners (and credit you by adding your URL profile so it can drive more profile visits to you), I would like to motive others to do what you just did! (Finish reading this guide) **Congratulations!**

FINAL WORDS (REVISED 2023 EDITION)

First, thank you for purchasing the Now You Know Guide. I know you could have picked any number of books to read about the online world, but you picked this one, and for that, I am extremely grateful.

I wrote the Now You Know Guidebook in 2020 as part of a crowdfunding project, fast forward to today:

These lessons have become a **Podcast** on Spotify, Applepodcast…(https://thenowyouknowpodcast.buzzsprout.com), **a successful course** at Temple University here in Japan and the NYK guidebook itself has been selling steady since it was launched. So, I am pretty happy about the outcome so far here.

That being said, the other side of the coin is that I have lost my LinkedIn account (I was banned for life and lost contact with my 300K+ listeners) my "crime"? went into polemic topics and suggested a different viewpoint during the height of the pandemic.

Anyway, as today (2023), many things are showing and pointing that perhaps my previous perspectives were not so irrational as LinkedIn managers (and its current owner, Mr. Gates) had portrayed. Lessons learned and I put in practice what I preach in this guidebook.

Thereafter, I have built my own platform (a simple website) https://flavio.online and I run a free weekly newsletter (Called "*From The Horse's Mouth Newsletter*") where I share a ton of memes (the best of the week in term of funny things I came across) together with some free thoughts.

So, if you are one of those that miss my comical posts on LinkedIn go ahead and catch up with me on my site.

Lastly, if you are into learning more about marketing (traditional or digital) check my two new social media presence: TikTok channel: https://www.tiktok.com/@fzmkt and YouTube channel: https://www.youtube.com/c/FZMKT

I post some to the point, short videos on those platforms on the marketing subject.

That's it. On this 2023 Edition, I have revised all the 101 lessons and updated a bit as needed. I also revised all the links (to make sure still works and added new ones).

So, what you have in your hands is the latest possible practical guidebook that will help you to succeed online in 2023 and way beyond.

That being said, if you enjoyed the Now You Know Guide and got some learnings from it, please take some time to post a review on Amazon and equally important, please also share the Now You Know Guide with someone who you think would benefit from it.

To help you on tracking the lending(s), I will add some lines below:

The Now You Know Guide Belongs To:

_____

(Write down your name above as the owner of the Now You Know guidebook)

Lending to: _____
    Date: _____
    After you finish reading it, please return to the
    owner.

Lending to: _____
    Date: _____
    After you finish reading it, please return to the
    owner.

Lending to: _____
    Date: _____
    After you finish reading it, please return to the
    owner.

Lending to: _____
    Date: _____
    After you finish reading it, please return to the
    owner.

Lending to: _____
    Date: _____
    After you finish reading it, please return to the
    owner.

I appreciate you for reading this guidebook as well as your support in spreading the word and this guide around!

10 RANDOM ONLINE FACTS: NOW YOU KNOW

1. The Internet was invented over 40 years ago, in a beer garden! Who says the best ideas don't come over a drink!

2. Interbrand invented the term "Wi-Fi" as a play on words of the term "Hi-Fi" or "High Fidelity". However, Wi-Fi doesn't actually stand for anything. What added to the confusion was the Wi-Fi Alliance's use of a nonsense advertising slogan, "The Standard for Wireless Fidelity," which led many people to think that Wi-Fi was an abbreviation of "Wireless Fidelity".

3. With the global average Internet speed sitting at 5.6Mbps, South Korea is storming ahead as the fastest country in the world, with an average Internet speed of 26.7Mbps!

4. Some of the strangest devices that connect to the Internet now include Walking Sticks, Umbrellas, Shirts, Water Bottles, Tails (for festival-goers) and Cutlery. I've left the particularly odd items off this list!

5. The term "surfing" the internet was coined in 1992 by an upstate New York librarian Jean Armour Polly, aka "Net Mom."

6. The first YouTube video was uploaded April 23, 2005. It's called "Me at the zoo," and features Jawed Karim, one of the founders, at the San Diego Zoo.

7. The first website is still online.
(http://info.cern.ch/hypertext/ WWW/TheProject.html)

8. The GIF format was invented by Steve Wilke, an engineer at CompuServe in 1987.

9. "Gangnam Style" by Psy is still the most-viewed YouTube video of all time. It's been viewed over three billion times and I am one of those viewers.

10. As of January 2023, there were 5.16 billion internet users worldwide, which is 64.4 percent of the global population. Of this total, 4.76 billion, or 59.4 percent of the world's population, were social media users.

For live statistics updates check: internetlivestats.com

RESOURCES:

I could do a whole book only on online resources that would help you on your online journey.

However, I want to make it relevant to what we have learned in the Now You Know Guide, so I will place here (in alphabetic order and revised for this edition) only the key references/tools I use often and can be helpful for you too.

PLANNING TOOLS:

Developing ideas for posts or sharing:

Bored Panda is a leading art and pop culture magazine viewed nearly 100 million times every month.
https://www.boredpanda.com

Giphy is your top source for the best & newest GIFs & Animated Stickers online.
https://giphy.com/

Google Trends: Trending searches on Google.
https://trends.google.com/

Hubspot Blog Topic Generator: Custom blog ideas.
https://www.hubspot.com/blog-topic-generator

Imgur is an American online image sharing Community.
https://imgur.com

Medium: Everyone's stories and ideas.
https://medium.com

Portent: Content idea generator.
https://www.portent.com/tools/title-maker/

Reddit is an American social news aggregation, web content rating, and discussion website.
https://www.reddit.com

Twitter is an American microblogging and social networking service on which users post and interact with messages known as "tweets". (It's especially useful for real-time events posts, check trending lists and use hashtags when you post)
https://twitter.com

CHECKING TOOLS:

Free Grammar Check
https://quillbot.com/grammar-check

ProWritingAid for professional authors who wanted to improve their manuscript before sending it to their editors.
https://prowritingaid.com

Grammarly: Finds & corrects mistakes of your writing.
https://www.grammarly.com

This free tool will analyze your headline to determine the Emotional Marketing Value (EMV) score based on proprietary analysis technology developed by Advanced Marketing Institute.
https://www.aminstitute.com/headline/

WRITING TOOLS:

Buzzsumo: Analyze what content performs best for any topic or competitor.
https://buzzsumo.com

ChatGPT is an artificial intelligence chatbot developed by OpenAI and released in November 2022.
https://chat.openai.com

Google Bard is Google's answer to ChatGPT and Bing's AI chat.
https://bard.google.com

Scrivener is a writing tool aimed at anyone working on a long document. It could be a novel, an essay, a pillar article, or a lengthy blog post.
https://www.literatureandlatte.com/scrivener/overview

Canva: **Amazingly** simple graphic design for bloggers.
https://www.canva.com

DALL·E 2 is an AI system that can create realistic images and art from a description in natural language.
https://labs.openai.com

Compressor.io is a powerful online tool for reducing drastically the size of your images and photos whilst maintaining a high quality with almost no difference before and after compression.
https://compressor.io

Dribbble: Dribbble search results for "freebie". An absolute freebie treasure.
https://dribbble.com

Fiverr is an online marketplace for freelance services…
Get 20% off on your first order with the link below:
http://www.fiverr.com/s2/6566400389

Easel.ly: Empowers anyone to create & share powerful visuals.
https://www.easel.ly

Egg Timer: Set a time and bookmark it for repeated use. (Helps you to dedicate a specific amount of your time on a writing task)
http://e.ggtimer.com

Freebbble: High-quality design freebies from Dribbble.
http://freebbble.com

Get UI Colors: Get awesome UI colors.
http://getuicolors.com

Hootsuite is a social media management tool (it used to be free but not anymore) that allows users to schedule and post updates.
https://hootsuite.com

Later is a free, easy-to-use platform for people or business looking to schedule photos and videos on their social media.
https://later.com

Meme Generator: The first online meme generator.
http://memegenerator.net

Pexels: Best free photos in one place.
https://www.pexels.com/

Pixabay: Free high-quality royalty-free images & stock.
https://pixabay.com

Placeit: Product mockups & templates.
https://placeit.net

Make beautiful quotes pictures with worry-free image license easily and free.
https://quotescover.com

TinyJPG | TinyPNG Compress simple images.
https://tinyjpg.com

Described as "a toolkit for storytellers", Unfold is an iOS and Android app that helps you create beautiful templates for Instagram stories. Bringing your creative visions to life is the driving idea behind Unfold. Find this app on Apple Store or/and Google Play Store.

INTERACTIONS TOOLS:

Brandwatch: Understand how consumers talk about your brand online with Brandwatch's data library of 1.4 trillion conversations (Paid).
https://www.brandwatch.com

Buffer: Tracks the follower activity and determining the perfect activity to schedule tweets to maximize your exposure.
https://buffer.com

TweetDeck: If you are an active Twitter user, look at TweetDeck. This management tool allows you to remove some of the noise, making the time you spend researching and engaging on the platform much more efficient.
https://tweetdeck.twitter.com

Hashtagsforlikes: Grow your following through the power of hashtags on Instagram
https://www.hashtagsforlikes.co/

Live Streaming Tools: You need a third-party broadcaster tool; some 3 popular options here:

Socialive (https://www.socialive.us),

Switcher Studio (https://www.switcherstudio.com)

and Restream (https://restream.io/).

Smart Social Media Monitoring Get instant access to mentions across social media, news, blogs, videos, forums, podcasts, reviews, and more.
https://brand24.com

"GOT TO EAT TOO" BONUS TOOLS

Amazon Influencer Program: Recommend Products and Get Rewarded.
https://affiliate-program.amazon.com/influencers

Fourstarzz: This platform is specially geared towards micro- and nano-influencers, so there's a good chance that you'll be able to get connected with a brand with ease.
https://www.fourstarzz.com

Mailchimp: Plan includes up to a maximum of 500 contacts. Select your audience size to calculate your price. The monthly email send limit for the Free plan is 1,000 sends (daily limit of 500).

(Creating a mail list for your listeners is always a good idea and can generate some revenues along the way) Newsletters plugins for your website too.
https://mailchimp.com

Pay Per Post is one of the larger services available that offer bloggers the opportunity to get paid for blogging about specific subjects. They are one of the pioneers of "paid to blog" opportunity-based marketplaces.
http://www.PayPerPost.com

Creating a domain:

Impossibility: The best domain name generator ever.
http://impossibility.org

Short Domain Search: Find short, available single-word domain names.
http://shortdomainsearch.com

Publishing eBooks:

Designrr is an online tool that creates beautiful eBooks or lead magnets from one or more web pages. It removes all the clutter like sidebars, social icons, adverts, navigation so you end up with pure, clean content in your book.
https://designrr.io/about/

And finally, Publishizer (I used them for crowdfunding this guidebook) They are a fundraising and literary agency that can help you crowdfund pre-order copies and land publishing deals. They guide you through creating your book proposal that the editorial team reviews for acceptance. You can then create your campaign, start marketing your book and offering bonuses and raise funds from readers during a 30-day period.

Pros

- Step-by-step guidance
- Connections with publishers
- Flexible publishing options

Cons

- Eventual royalties vary
- Short 30-day campaign deadline
- Signing deals take time

https://publishizer.com

Note: In case of any link stops to work, just google it.

ABOUT THE AUTHOR

(Who's this guy anyway?)

Flavio Souza is a life explorer, an award-winning entrepreneur, marketer, professor, technology advocate, writer and a believer in the human race.

He has over 30 years of experience working in marketing and hi-tech business areas at global corporations in his native Brazil, Europe and Japan.

Today, he lives in Tokyo, loves Yubari melon and runs a Japanese digital agency with an array of sites with heavy daily traffic visitors coming to learn about the latest techie trends as well as be refreshed with some positive news and vibes.

You can find Flavio by visiting: https://flavio.online
and on YouTube, TikTok (@fzmkt) and Twitter (@FZ_mkt)

www.ingramcontent.com/pod-product-compliance
Lightning Source LLC
Chambersburg PA
CBHW070346220526
45467CB00001B/270